CELEBRATE
Every Day

CELEBRATE
Every Day

RECIPES FOR MAKING THE MOST OF SPECIAL MOMENTS WITH YOUR FAMILY

JAIME RICHARDSON
creator of Sophistimom.com

skirt!

Guilford, Connecticut
An imprint of Globe Pequot Press

To buy books in quantity for corporate use
or incentives, call **(800) 962-0973**
or e-mail **premiums@GlobePequot.com**.

skirt!® is an attitude . . . spirited, independent, outspoken, serious, playful
and irreverent, sometimes controversial, always passionate.

skirt!® is an imprint of Globe Pequot Press.
skirt!® is a registered trademark of Morris Publishing Group, LLC,
and is used with express permission.

All photos by Jaime Richardson, except author photo on
page 224 by Erin Summerill Photography

Project Editor: David Legere
Text Design: Sheryl P. Kober
Layout Artist: Melissa Evarts

Library of Congress Cataloging-in-Publication data is available on file.

ISBN 978-0-7627-8234-5

Printed in the United States of America

10 9 8 7 6 5 4 3 2 1

contents

acknowledgments

In years to come, I will look back on this book as the culmination and token of my early years as a single mom. I was a work in progress before I started, and still am. Despite that, dozens of people, both friends and family, have believed in me, and to them I want to extend my deepest gratitude:

Mary Norris, my editor, and the tireless team at Globe Pequot Press who have turned my words and pictures into something beautiful.

Amy Moore-Benson, my agent, who was interested in seeing what I could come with up after seeing my blog on an iPad with a sluggish internet connection, and then remembering me six months later, when I finally got up the courage to ask if she'd represent me.

Timothy Robinson, who listened to me the very first time I ever breathed the words, "I'm thinking of writing a cookbook," to someone in publishing, and then pointed me in the right direction.

Connie and Grant McKenzie, my good friends who insisted, on a weekly basis, I should write this book in the first place.

Josh Mormann, my big brother, for believing in me and being the backbone of Sophistimom.com. I could not have done one scrap of any of this without his help.

Jessica Mormann, my sister, whom I still look up to, for her words of wisdom and countless pep talks.

Julie Donaldson, my writing buddy, fellow traveler, and cherished friend. She was always there—always—to offer support, suggestions, encouragement, and a kick in the pants whenever I needed it.

Erin Summerill, my photography consultant, writing conspirator, partner in dieting, and wingman. Without even knowing it, she has lifted me out of some of the darkest times of my life.

The Provo City Library—most particularly Laura Wadley—whose suggestions of books and music helped to shape and define each party into something special.

Shannon and Scott Bingham, for the use of their gorgeous home, and their patience and help while I finished the book.

Kamran Siddiqi, a fellow blogger, and the most talented kid I know, for his encouraging words and insights, and for his help with the Indian recipes.

Lila Tueller, for the use of her beautiful quilts.

Stacey Ann Ratliff, for going above and beyond friendship to test so many of my recipes.

Jessie Humphries, for putting me on the spot, and making me talk to Amy, who is now my agent.

The people at Weck Jars for providing all the beautiful jam jars, flasks, and tumblers in the book.

Angie and Bert Lewis, for being there for me, time and time again.

My mother. I could not have asked for a better one. She is my biggest supporter, and unfailing confidante. I can never get over how lucky I am to have her as a mom.

And finally, and most importantly, my kids: Stuart, Sophie, and Charlie. I love you guys, with all my heart. Thank you, thank you, thank you for being my light, my joy, and the very best parts of my life. This book never would have happened without you and your beautiful faces.

introduction

My poor kids had no idea what they were in for when they got me for a mom.

When my oldest was born, I began reading *Peter Pan* to him before we left the hospital. Not long after that, I decided *Pride and Prejudice* would be required reading before my daughters (yet to be born) would ever leave the house on a date. And then there's my youngest son, whose middle name is as dreamy as a Jane Austen hero's.

When life began in our house, I was quite determined to raise two princes and a princess fit to inhabit my castle in the sky. They would love not only classic literature, but all other fine things of life: great food, foreign countries and languages, art, philosophy, logic, and architecture. Classical music.

But then the inevitable happened: Reality prevailed.

Things like Shakespeare and eggs Benedict quickly took backseats to things like Spongebob and Gogurt as my kids' preferences won out, and I saw how much easier it was to let certain things go.

Even so, I did try to stuff as much sophistication into the gaps as I could. Sometimes it was dancing together in the kitchen while arias by Mozart and Bach played on full blast; other times it was teaching my toddlers the lyrics to Nat King Cole songs. We read classics together as often as we could, and I introduced them to crème brûlée. They thought I was a genius.

However, many—if not most—of my attempts at bringing them up well were not as happily received as I would have hoped, especially surrounding food. My three-year-old, for example, wouldn't eat pasta. Honestly, what kind of kid doesn't like pasta?

So I did what every other woman of my demographic was doing at the time: I started a blog. I figured, if my kids wouldn't eat the lasagna, someone else's kid in the world would. I called

it Sophistimom, and it became my place to tell funny stories, create new recipes, share our favorite books, and relate my attempts to teach the kids good manners, and anything else a respectable person should know.

Not long after I started, though, I found myself single. Whenever I look back at that time, I have trouble understanding how I had the tenacity to keep going with the blog. But I realize now how important Sophistimom was to me at the time. Besides giving me goals and purpose, it was something colorful and energetic to dance in my mind's periphery while I attended to darker affairs.

That first summer, while I was really in the thick of things, Brooke McLay, who is a friend and fellow blogger, had an idea to go on a picnic with our two families. She found an idyllic location, and we divided up the food arrangements. Because we both put our best into the outing, we shared something quite magical with our kids. As we celebrated our friendship, I discovered the importance of stopping to do something meaningful and wonderful, even in the midst of trials.

That day the problems of our life were still scratching relentlessly at the windowpane. But we ignored them. We took a quiet afternoon with loved ones, and celebrated our time together.

And as my family's new life unfolds, we keep finding more moments like these. We love to throw parties when we've just finished reading a book together, with some sort of food that ties in with the story or the era. Sometimes, it's an author's or an artist's birthday, and we take a chance at creating something in his or her style. Other times, it's an impromptu picnic on a Sunday afternoon, with simply the food we find in the fridge.

We've created treasured occasions with just the four of us, something I may have thought impossible a couple of years ago. We've learned things don't have to be too elaborate, and we certainly don't need to impress the neighbors. It's more about figuring out how to make our time together special.

Because, celebrating really isn't about events, it's about the moments—what you learn from them, and how you feel. Celebrating is about cherishing the significant moments set aside from everything else—the moments that engrave themselves on your memories. Perhaps it is a smile, or an uninterrupted conversation. Maybe it is the feel of a toddler's hand, warm and soft inside your own. It doesn't matter if you're serving a feast on a national holiday or just reveling in the first time your kid remembers to throw his dirty socks in the laundry. If you can grab those moments and look at them—hold them up to the light and find joy in them—then you've just found something worthy of celebrating.

This book is how my kids and I celebrate on the best of days—with treasured books, inspired music, and of course, great food.

What I Want You to Take Away from this Book

In this book you will find twenty celebrations organized by season, each featuring delicious recipes, suggestions for books to read and share, party music suggestions, and ideas on how to involve your children with each celebration. I hope it will inspire you to celebrate with your own families in simple, lovely ways.

The very last thing I want it to do is stress you out.

When I was first married, I was the queen of letting something like this stress me out. I would have thought that I needed to follow every menu of each party to a tee. Then I would have stressed out that I didn't have the right stand mixer, the proper kitchen tools, or the appropriate plates or jars.

But I hope you'll read this book differently. Let it give you ideas, but not overwhelm you. Paramount to all other ideas

in here is the idea of being together as a family. If celebrating a moment with your kids means ordering a pizza instead of spending all day in the kitchen, do it! Then use the time you saved to give more hugs and take a few more seconds to look into your children's eyes.

spring

welcome spring brunch

When I was growing up, the promise of spring always began with crocuses peeking out of the dirt near our breezeway door. I would watch over them, bundled in my winter coat, and dream of the warmer weather that was sure to come soon. But spring in Massachusetts started with big promises, followed by many cold weeks and usually snow. And then before I knew it, it was summer.

Depending on where my kids and I have lived over the years, spring has been either cold and gray—more like a long thaw than anything else—or hot and hurried, as if it had no intention of being there at all. Occasionally we've lived in places where the spring came and actually wanted to be there. But even then, the season was often trampled under the rush of after-school sports and the last few weeks of classes.

In any case, spring can be as hard to hold on to as a fleeting thought. It's a delicate season, and very unpredictable. You really have to watch and wait for it, and welcome it when it comes.

The beauty of having these little parties for my own family is that most of them can happen at the last minute. For our Welcome Spring Brunch, we prepared quite a few things in advance so we would be ready when that optimal spring day came. But, we also planned on not knowing some specifics. I knew if we counted on having it outdoors, it was sure to rain or be too windy. As we prepared, we decided we would set up a table of food inside the house and eat it wherever made

RECIPES:

Nectarine and Strawberry
  Smoothies
Oeufs en Cocotte *on Toast with*
  Lox and Dill
Lemon Wreath
Carrot Cake Muffins with Cream
  Cheese Frosting

get creative:

Set up easels in the backyard and have the children do their own paintings of what springtime means to them. Provide them with watercolors or gouache.

sense at the time. We made the muffins and frosting ahead of time and froze them, then had a list ready to go of the foods we'd need to buy right before the party.

I can't think of any composer more fitting for this celebration than Vivaldi. His works are so full of energy and promise —perfect for spring. We chose his Flautino Concerto in C and, of course, "Spring" from *The Four Seasons*. As we listened to the music, and after finishing our brunch, we got out some small pots and planted seeds. I put the children in charge of choosing which kinds of plants they wanted to grow, and learning how to plant them from the instructions on the seed packets. After the seeds were planted and carefully placed on our windowsill, my daughter read aloud Beatrix Potter's *The Tale of Peter Rabbit*.

No matter what your weather is like, you can celebrate the promise of the season. If it rains, put on some galoshes and stomp in some puddles before coming inside for the brunch. Or, if that last layer of snow just hasn't melted yet, pop in Aaron Copeland's *Appalachian Spring*, crank up the volume, and get everyone to close his or her eyes to imagine that it's spring.

books to inspire:

The Tale of Peter Rabbit, by Beatrix Potter
Make Way for Ducklings, by Robert McCloskey
Trumpet of the Swan, by E. B. White

Nectarine and Strawberry Smoothies

The beauty of making smoothies is that you can get creative and not follow a strict recipe. I like to start with a plain yogurt and a fruit juice with no added sugar, and then toss in whatever fruit I have in the fridge. For our brunch, I happened to have strawberries and nectarines, but you can tweak this recipe however you like. SERVES 6

Place all the ingredients in a blender and pulse until smooth, adding more juice or fruit as desired.

4 nectarines, cleaned and pitted

10 large strawberries, washed, with leaves and stems removed

1 cup Greek yogurt

2 cups 100% fruit juice, such as white grape or apple

Oeufs en Cocotte on Toast with Lox and Dill

Oeufs en Cocotte are eggs baked in cream. Whenever I eat them (and I can't that often or I'd have hips the size of a large inner tube), I remember my reason for living. They're sweet and rich and silky all at the same time. Absolutely transcendent.

I first learned how to make these from watching Ina Garten on The Barefoot Contessa, *who makes hers in a broiler. Every oven's broiler is different, so although I give cooking times in this recipe, they are only approximate. You will need to watch the eggs carefully to determine which cooking time will work for your own oven.* SERVES 6

6 slices artisan bread

6 eggs

¼ cup heavy cream

1 teaspoon butter

½ teaspoon dry dill weed

Kosher salt and pepper

4 ounces lox or smoked salmon

Fleur de sel or another coarse, mild salt for garnish

1. Preheat oven to 400°F. Place bread slices on a cookie sheet and toast in the oven for 10 minutes, or until starting to turn golden brown around the edges.

2. Crack eggs into a small bowl, making sure all the yolks are intact.

3. Place an oven rack in the top third of the oven. Turn broiler on high. Pour cream into a 10-inch broiler-safe pan, such as an enamel-coated cast-iron skillet, or a broiler-safe casserole dish. Dot the top with butter. Set over medium heat, and cook until the cream starts to bubble.

4. Carefully slide in the eggs, making sure to keep their yolks intact. Sprinkle with dill and a pinch of kosher salt and pepper. Cook on the stovetop until the egg whites start to change from clear to white around the edges, about 2 minutes. Transfer the skillet to the oven and broil for 2–4 minutes, until the egg whites are completely set and the yolks are as soft or as firm as you like.*

5. Use a spatula to slide each egg onto a piece of toast. Top with salmon and a sprinkling of fleur de sel.

*Important: In this recipe, I always use extremely fresh eggs, and usually cook them until the yolks are soft and not fully cooked. However, eating undercooked eggs can cause food-borne illness, especially for very young children, pregnant women, the elderly, or anyone whose health is compromised. If you have any doubts, please cook your eggs thoroughly.

Lemon Wreath

I find lemon desserts to be sublime. As a bread this could be considered a dessert or a breakfast food, and can therefore be enjoyed any time of the day. MAKES 1 LARGE LOAF

3 cups all-purpose flour

1 package (1 scant tablespoon) instant yeast

1 cup warm milk (110°F)

1 egg yolk

3 tablespoons melted butter

2 tablespoons brown rice syrup or honey

¾ teaspoon kosher salt

1 cup sugar

Zest of 2 lemons

4 tablespoons salted butter, at room temperature

Lemon Cream Cheese Glaze (recipe follows)

1. In the bowl of an electric mixer fitted with the dough hook, mix together flour and yeast.* Pour in water along with milk and egg yolk, melted butter, brown rice syrup, and salt. Knead on low for 10 minutes, or until dough is smooth and elastic.

2. Place dough in a buttered bowl, and cover with a clean kitchen towel. Place in a warm, draft-free place until doubled in size, about 30–45 minutes.

3. While the dough rises, place sugar and lemon zest in a food processor fitted with the steel blade, and pulse until sugar is pale yellow.

4. Line a large baking sheet with a piece of parchment paper. Turn out dough onto a well-floured board and roll out into a large rectangle, about 18 x 12 inches.

5. Spread salted butter all over the surface of the dough, and sprinkle with lemon sugar. Roll up the long way, then pinch along the seam to seal in the lemon sugar.

*The method of mixing yeast and flour together is a risky move if the yeast you have has been sitting around awhile. If you know your packet of yeast is new, then proceed with the recipe. If you have any doubts, proof your yeast by stirring it together with the warm milk and a drop of honey. If after a few minutes the yeast mixture starts to bubble, you're good to go. Just add it in with the rest of the wet ingredients, and follow the remainder of the recipe. If your yeast does not bubble, it is no longer active, and you need a new packet.

6. Place the roll on the prepared baking sheet, and form into a ring. Pinch the dough where the two ends meet to form a seal. Using kitchen shears, make cuts perpendicular to the center, three-fourths of the way to the center of the ring. Repeat every 1½ inches all the way around the ring, twisting each cut section on its side so the swirl is facing up. Cover and let rise 30 minutes.

7. Preheat oven to 350°F. Use wide strips of aluminum foil to loosely cover the outer portion of the ring. Bake for 15 minutes, until the center of the ring starts to brown. Remove the foil, and continue to bake for 10–15 minutes, or until the edges start to brown and the bread sounds hollow when rapped with a wooden spoon. Remove from oven.

8. Allow bread to cool on the baking sheet for several minutes. Use the parchment paper to transfer to a serving platter, tear off the excess paper, and drizzle with Lemon Cream Cheese Glaze.

Lemon Cream Cheese Glaze

Place all the ingredients in a bowl. With an electric beater, beat together until smooth.

2 ounces cream cheese, at room temperature

2 tablespoons butter, at room temperature

2 tablespoons lemon juice

Zest of 1 lemon

1 cup powdered sugar

Carrot Cake Muffins with Cream Cheese Frosting

Oh, how I love these muffins. They are bursting with flavor, and when they're made with whole-wheat flour, they can nearly be considered healthy. We love to freeze the leftovers individually. Then, with a twenty-second zap in the microwave, we have an instant, on-the-go breakfast. MAKES 1 DOZEN MUFFINS

1 cup raisins

1 cup light brown sugar

1 teaspoon white wine vinegar

2 eggs

⅔ cup vegetable oil or light-colored olive oil

1 teaspoon pure vanilla extract

1¼ cups whole-wheat pastry flour or all-purpose flour

1 teaspoon baking powder

½ teaspoon baking soda

¾ teaspoon salt

½ teaspoon ground cinnamon

¼ teaspoon ground cloves

¼ teaspoon ground ginger

1 pound carrots, peeled and grated

Cream Cheese Frosting (recipe follows)

1. Preheat oven to 350°F. Line a standard muffin tin with 12 paper liners. Place raisins in a small bowl and cover with 1 cup boiling water. Set aside.

2. In the bowl of an electric mixer fitted with the whisk attachment, combine brown sugar, vinegar, eggs, oil, and vanilla. Scrape down the bowl to ensure everything is well incorporated. Raise speed to medium-high and beat mixture until smooth, fluffy, and sugar is dissolved, about 2 minutes.

3. In a medium bowl, whisk together flour, baking powder, baking soda, salt, and spices. Add carrots. Drain raisins and add to the dry ingredients and carrots. Toss the carrots and raisins in the flour mixture until well coated.

4. Stir the carrot mixture into the oil and sugar mixture, and mix until well incorporated. Do not overmix. Divide batter evenly among the muffin liners.

5. Bake for 20–25 minutes, or until a toothpick inserted into the center muffins comes out clean. Allow to cool completely, then frost with Cream Cheese Frosting.

variations on a theme:

Take a field trip to a local nursery, or even a talented (and friendly) neighbor's house, and have the gardener take you on a tour to see all the plants. Call ahead to make the necessary arrangements.

Cream Cheese Frosting

1. Cream butter and cream cheese together with an electric mixer set to low speed.

2. Add sugar, extracts, and cream. Raise speed to medium-high and beat until smooth and fluffy.

4 tablespoons unsalted butter, at room temperature

4 ounces cream cheese, at room temperature

1 cup confectioner's sugar

½ teaspoon pure vanilla extract

½ teaspoon pure almond extract

1 teaspoon heavy cream

world traveler party

There used to be a time when we could fly for free. As the family of an airline pilot, all we needed was a flight that had a few open seats, and off we could go. We loved going to Boston at least once or twice a year, and enjoyed exploring different cities around the country—Portland, Traverse City, San Francisco. I once took off by myself for a weeklong trip to England and got to fly first class on the way there. They gave me hot towels and three-course meals. And my seat converted into a bed.

Ah. Those were the days.

Now I wish I could use those flight benefits to show my kids the world. First on my list to see are Australia and New Zealand, and then on to Germany or France. I thought Scandinavia might be nice at Christmastime some year, and, of course, we would have to travel to Italy and spend a whole month.

Even though we haven't seen those places yet, for now, we will dream.

I can't think of a better book to inspire the inner jet-setter than *Around the World in Eighty Days.* That was the starting point of our celebration. We read it together, and then chose a country Phileas Fogg passes through on his journey.

Since my oldest son and I love Indian food, we picked it to feature for our party. We decided on a simple menu, with just a small sampling of a few favorite Indian foods. Then we went online for inspiration. A fellow blogger tweeted some suggestions of where we could find decorations, which we ran out and bought that afternoon. Then we wrapped my daughter in

get creative:

Watch a foreign film together such as *The Red Balloon* (*Le Ballon Rouge*), *Ponyo*, or *A Town Called Panic* (*Panique au Village*)

some sari fabric, and we gathered over our meal of mulligatawny, chicken coconut korma, rice, and roti.

For your own World Traveler Party, you can make your celebration as elaborate or as simple as you like. You could highlight India as we did, or you could choose another country your family is interested in. You might even pick a place with ancestral ties. Children's sections of good libraries are filled with nonfiction on locations that you may not find as easily at the bookstore. Ask your librarian for suggestions on reading material related to the country you've chosen. Once you've collected your information, celebrate with food and decorations typical of the locale.

Mango Lassis

Kamran Siddiqi, the author of The Sophisticated Gourmet blog (www.sophisticatedgourmet.com), is one of my favorite people. This is his Mango Lassi recipe, which I've adapted slightly.

Blend all the ingredients in a blender until smooth. Pour into fancy glasses and serve.

3 cups milk

2 cups plain yogurt

¼ cup agave nectar

2 ripe mangoes, peeled and cut into chunks

Juice and zest of 1 lime

2 cups crushed ice

books to inspire:

Around the World in Eighty Days, by Jules Verne
How I Learned Geography, by Uri Shulevitz
While You Are Sleeping: A Lift-the-Flap Book of Time Around the World, by Durga Bernhard

Mulligatawny

Mulligatawny, which means "pepper water" in Tamil, is not authentic Indian cuisine, but we love it anyway. My son and I agree it's like eating the best part of a good curry, without the rice or the meat. It's simply all the flavor in a bowl.

I use canned chicken stock or chicken broth when I make this, but you could also use a good vegetable stock to make it vegan. You can also make this soup ahead and freeze it. SERVES 6

1. Heat the oil in a large pot set over medium heat. Add onions and salt, and cook until translucent and starting to brown, about 10 minutes.

2. Stir in garlic, spices, and tomato, and sauté until spices are fragrant and tomato is heated through. Add lentils, tomato paste, ginger, and apple chunks, and cook 1 minute more.

3. Stir in chicken broth, and bring to a boil. Reduce heat to medium-low, and let simmer for 30 minutes, or until apple chunks are tender to the point of a knife.

4. Use an immersion blender to puree soup until smooth. If you don't have an immersion blender, place about 2 cups of soup at a time in a traditional blender, cover with the lid and a kitchen towel, and blend until smooth. Repeat with remaining soup. Return to the pot. Add water if necessary to achieve desired consistency. Stir in lemon juice, and simmer on low until ready to serve. Garnish with cilantro.

1 tablespoon olive oil

1 medium yellow onion, finely diced

Pinch of kosher salt

4 cloves garlic, minced

1 teaspoon ground cumin

1 teaspoon Madras curry powder

1 large tomato, chopped

½ cup red lentils

¼ cup tomato paste

1 inch fresh ginger, peeled and grated

1 Granny Smith apple, peeled and cut into ½-inch chunks

2 (14.5-ounce) cans chicken broth, or 4 cups chicken stock

Juice of ½ lemon

Cilantro, chopped or left in sprigs, for garnish

variations on a theme:

Can't decide on just one country? Have each child pick a country he or she is interested in, look it up at the library or in an online encyclopedia, and find out basic information about each place. Then for the party, make a sampling of foods from each, such as souvlaki from Greece, miso soup from Japan, and gelato from Italy. You'll all learn, and laugh, a lot.

Chicken Coconut Korma

I pieced this recipe together from multiple versions I found on the Internet, along with the suggestions of Kamran Siddiqi and his Grandmum. Once I took the first bite, I felt like singing for joy.

I learned that the secret to this recipe is the onion puree, which, when cooked right, lends a sweetness to the dish without adding fruit or sugar. It's a tear-jerking job, though, so if anyone in the family wears contacts, you might want to put them in charge. They just might have an easier go of it. SERVES 4-6

1 pound chicken breast, cut into 1-inch chunks

1 cup plain Greek yogurt

1 inch fresh ginger, peeled and grated

1 medium yellow onion, peeled and chopped into 8 large pieces

Pinch of red pepper flakes

3 tablespoons ghee, or 2 tablespoons butter with 1 tablespoon olive oil

1 teaspoon Madras curry powder

½ teaspoon kosher salt

4 cloves garlic, grated or pressed through a garlic press

1 cup coconut milk

1 tablespoon freshly squeezed lemon juice

⅛ teaspoon garam masala

Sliced almonds, for garnish

Cilantro, chopped or left in sprigs, for garnish

1. Stir together chicken pieces, yogurt, and grated ginger. Cover and refrigerate for 5–6 hours, or overnight if possible.

2. Place the onion and red pepper flakes in a food processor fitted with the steel blade attachment. Pulse until onions become a smooth puree. (Alternately, puree the onion and red pepper flakes in a blender with ¼ cup water that will cook out later.)

3. Melt ghee in a large skillet set over medium-low heat, and add curry powder. Cook for 2 minutes, or until fragrant. Add onion puree and salt, and sauté, stirring frequently, until onions are tender and starting to brown, about 5–6 minutes. If the onion puree becomes too dry as it cooks, add a tablespoon or two of water.

4. Stir in garlic and chicken (with the marinade), and cook until chicken whitens around the edges. Add coconut milk, and simmer for 10 minutes, or until chicken is cooked through. The sauce should be about the thickness of a watery tomato sauce, but will vary depending on the type of yogurt and coconut milk used. (If it is too thick, add some water a little bit at a time until you achieve the desired consistency. If the sauce is too thin, remove chicken to a plate with a slotted spoon, and simmer the sauce until it is reduced to a thickness to your liking. Return chicken to the sauce, cover, and simmer at a very low heat for 10 minutes more.)

5. Stir in lemon juice and garam masala, and serve with a garnish of almond slices and cilantro.

Roti

Roti is a flatbread with thin layers, the perfect vehicle for eating curry. My roommate taught me how to make it when I was in college, and several more people have instructed me since then, with a different recipe every time. My version is a combination of all of them.

But I will let you in on a little secret: Whenever I am too lazy to make roti, I just pick up some all-natural uncooked flour tortillas from the refrigerator section of the grocery store and follow the instructions on the package. They save me some time, and are almost as tasty. But shhh . . . don't tell anyone. MAKES 10

2 cups unbleached all-purpose flour, plus more for rolling

½ teaspoon baking powder

½ teaspoon kosher salt

1 tablespoon vegetable oil, plus more for rubbing

¾ cup warm water

2 tablespoons ghee or melted butter

1. In a large bowl, combine flour, baking powder, and salt. Stir in oil and use clean hands to mix until oil is well incorporated into the flour mixture. Add water and stir until it combines evenly. Knead into a cohesive ball and rub with oil. Cover and let rest for 10 minutes.

2. Divide the dough into 10 equal pieces, and roll into balls.

3. Set a large nonstick skillet over medium heat. Dip a ball of dough in flour and roll it out into an 8-inch circle. Place in the skillet and cook until bubbled and golden on one side, and then flip and cook until browned on the other side. Brush with ghee or melted butter. Place on an oven-safe plate in a warm oven—200°F—until ready to serve. Repeat with the remaining balls of dough.

I only buy fresh ginger about once a year. When I find a good batch of it at the grocery store, I buy a few pieces, tie up the bag, and throw it in the door of my freezer. It's there whenever I need some for a recipe. It grates beautifully when frozen, but if I ever need to defrost a piece, I simply break off what I need and run it under warm water. It's then ready to go.

movie night

I might just be one of those overprotective parents, the kind I swore I'd never be back when I knew nothing about parenting. I have to say I get a little nervous when the kids are out of my sight, even now that they're older. The truth is, I just like to have them home with me—right where I can reach out and put my arm around them or touch their faces. When they're safe, I feel safe, and everything feels right in the world.

Our family movie nights started when we lived across the street from a playground. The other parents in the neighborhood would let their kids play there well past dusk, and I needed an incentive I could use to pull my own kids inside and get them to bed at a reasonable hour. Bribery is always a good parenting strategy, so I would lure them into the house with popcorn, let them set up sleeping bags in one of their rooms, and watch a DVD on the laptop. It has become a solid tradition.

Even though movie nights involve staring at a screen, they're still an opportunity to draw closer as a family. For me, it's a chance to slow down and see my children in a way I don't see them in our normal day-to-day activities. What they laugh at is always revealing, and I am usually surprised at their social understanding. When we laugh at the same line of a movie, and then quote it to each other later, we're building a collection of "inside jokes" that bind us intellectually. And I love that. It helps us create a legacy of friendship that will last far beyond the years they live at home.

Though our movie nights are generally quite simple, with just a DVD and maybe some popcorn, for this particular evening we went all out with sandwiches, soda floats, popcorn, and movie candy. We chose a movie that tied into a book we had just finished reading, snuggled into our pajamas, and curled up on the couch.

For your movie night celebration, choose a show that everyone will enjoy, adults included. Then make your celebration as simple or as elaborate as you want.

RECIPES:
Baguette Muffalettas
Flavored Popcorn
Soda Floats
Homemade Snow Caps

music to inspire:
Soundtrack from *The Wizard of Oz* or the film you choose to feature for the evening

Baguette Muffalettas

Muffalettas are Sicilian sandwiches made famous in New Orleans. They feature an olive salad spread and are made on great loaves of round bread. I put mine on baguettes to make them easier to hold.
MAKES 4–6 SANDWICHES

Olive Tapenade (recipe follows)

1 French baguette, sliced in half lengthwise

1 tablespoon extra-virgin olive oil

Several slices of Italian meats, such as pepperoni, salami, and ham

4 slices Provolone cheese, each cut in half

1. Spread the Olive Tapenade on one half of the bread, and drizzle the olive oil on the other half. Layer the bread with the meats and cheese.

2. Slice into 4–6 sandwich-size wedges and serve.

Olive Tapenade

¼ cup pitted green olives with pimentos

¼ cup pitted kalamata olives

1 tablespoon sun-dried tomatoes

1 teaspoon red wine vinegar

2 teaspoons extra-virgin olive oil

Pinch of salt

Pulse all the ingredients in a food processor until roughly chopped.

books to inspire:

The Wizard of Oz, by Frank Baum
Matilda, by Roald Dahl
The Princess Bride, by William Goldman
The Invention of Hugo Cabret, by Brian Selznick

Flavored Popcorn

My favorite way to salt popcorn is to use kosher salt or sea salt that has been ground into a fine powder using a food processor or coffee grinder. Most movie nights, we just pour a little bit of melted salted butter over our air-popped popcorn and follow it with a pinch of this superfine salt.

When we want our popcorn to be extra special, we sprinkle on the following flavor combinations.

Italian Popcorn Seasoning

MAKES ENOUGH FOR UP TO 10 BATCHES OF POPCORN

Pulse all the ingredients together in a coffee grinder until fine. Pour 2 tablespoons of melted butter over 8 cups of popcorn, and sprinkle with a few pinches of the Italian popcorn seasoning. Store remaining seasoning in the refrigerator for another occasion.

2 teaspoons kosher salt

4 teaspoons Italian seasoning

¼ teaspoon garlic powder

⅛ teaspoon onion powder

3 tablespoons grated Parmesan or Romano cheese

Sugar and Spice Popcorn Seasoning

MAKES ENOUGH FOR 3 BATCHES OF POPCORN

Grind sugar, salt, and spices in a coffee grinder until fine. Pour into a small bowl, and mix with vanilla. Pour 2–3 tablespoons of melted butter over 8 cups of popcorn and sprinkle with one or more tablespoons of seasoning. Refrigerate remaining mixture to save for future use.

6 tablespoons sugar

½ teaspoon kosher salt or sea salt

¼ teaspoon ground nutmeg

1 teaspoon ground cinnamon

¼ teaspoon pure vanilla extract

get creative:

Put popcorn in red-and-white-striped bags—available at party supply stores—and place candy in small boxes. Encourage the children to set up a concession stand and ticket booth. If it's a film you really want to showcase, decorate the family room like a scene from the movie. For example, you could put yellow paper on the floor and hang green paper lanterns for *The Wizard of Oz*.

Soda Floats

This is the easiest dessert of all time. If ever I am late for a party, I just stop at the store to buy fruit sodas and vanilla ice cream. I dish these out once I arrive, and no one is ever disappointed. SERVES 8

2 pints good-quality vanilla ice
  cream

4 (16-ounce) bottles fruit soda
  in assorted flavors

Place a scoop of ice cream in the bottom of each glass and slowly cover it with soda. As the bubbles settle, top off with more soda. Serve with a spoon and a straw.

Homemade Snow Caps

This is a very easy, very quick candy that's just like what you'd get at the theater. MAKES 1 CUP CANDY

1. Place chocolate chips in a disposable pastry bag or sturdy plastic ziplock bag. Microwave on high for 20 seconds, then knead the chocolate with your hands. Microwave again for 10 seconds, and knead again. Repeat until the chocolate is completely melted.

2. Line a large baking sheet with parchment paper. Use scissors to cut a very small opening on the end of the pastry bag or on one of the corners of the ziplock bag. (You may need to experiment with the size of the opening a little bit to get the chocolate to come out the way you want.) Squeeze drops of the melted chocolate—about the size of large chocolate chips—onto the parchment-lined baking sheet. Sprinkle with nonpareils. Refrigerate for 20 minutes, or until set.

1 cup good-quality semi-sweet chocolate chips

1 ounce white nonpareils

variations on a theme:

If the weather is warm, hang a white sheet on the back of the house or from a clothesline strung across the yard. Find a projector to play the movie, and invite the neighbors.

woodland picnic

Growing up, our neighborhood was a dozen homes scattered amongst pine trees and a network of ponds. Living things were everywhere—honeybees, snapping turtles, woodpeckers, owls, and egrets. While I stayed close to home picking flowers and experimenting in the kitchen, my naturalist brother would spend hours roaming the woods with his dog, exploring the local ponds and cranberry bogs.

I can't quite figure out why my kids' lives are protected and harried when my own childhood was unhurried and free. I often wish I could raise them where I grew up so they could learn as I did, by wandering and exploring. But with the way the world is now, I don't feel as comfortable as my own mother did when she left us alone for hours. My children have cell phones so that I can call to check in every twenty minutes.

Either the world isn't as safe as it used to be, or I'm neurotic. Even if my children never have the chance to live where I grew up, however, we can still celebrate the woods.

My children and I live in the Rocky Mountains, so for us, a woodland picnic means heading into higher elevations. As we ascended on this particular occasion, we listened to *The Carnival of the Animals. VII. Aquarium* by Saint-Saëns in the car. It sounds like the music you'd hear in a fairyland.

After a short hike, we found a clearing in a cluster of quaking aspens, and spread a blanket for our picnic. A few days earlier, the children did research in the library to find out about the local plants and wildlife. Once we arrived,

RECIPES:
Feta and Spinach Purses
Leek and Cream Cheese Quiche
Buttermilk Panna Cotta with
  Blackberries
Brown Sugar Amaretti

music to set the scene:
The Carnival of the Animals. VII. Aquarium, by Camille Saint-Saëns
Peter and the Wolf, by Sergei Prokofiev
Scottish Fantasy, by Max Bruch
Peer Gynt Suite, no. 1, op. 46, by Edvard Grieg

variations on a
theme:

Pick any natural outdoor
setting if no woods
are nearby, such as a
meadow, park, beach, or
country field.

they were able to point out and identify many of the different leaves and bugs. Then, we let our imaginations roam like Wendy Darling's in *Peter Pan*. We took turns telling fairy stories, inspired by the woods around us.

To have your own Woodland Picnic, venture to a natural setting such as a meadow, a country field, or even a city park. Have your children research the area's flora and fauna. Bring colored pencils and field notebooks for the children so they can sketch and take notes on their findings. Then encourage them to make believe the kinds of enchanting creatures that could live in such a setting, hidden away from humans.

get creative:

Make your own field notebook. Gather a small stack of unbleached paper, fold it in half, and staple along the fold, or use a needle and twine to sew the binding. Have children sketch and write about their findings, both what they observe with their senses and what they sense with their imaginations.

Feta and Spinach Purses

These purses are just a fun variation on the classic Greek spanakopita. MAKES 8 PURSES

1 tablespoon good olive oil

1 small yellow onion, finely
diced

1 pound baby spinach, washed
and dried

¼ teaspoon freshly ground
nutmeg

Pinch of cayenne pepper

4 ounces feta cheese, crumbled

Kosher salt and pepper

1 egg, lightly beaten

1 teaspoon freshly squeezed
lemon juice (optional)

1 package phyllo

1 stick (8 tablespoons) salted
butter, melted

2 leek leaves, torn in long,
¼-inch strips (for tying the
purses)

1. In a large high-sided skillet, heat olive oil over medium heat.
Add onion and cook, stirring occasionally, until tender and
turning golden brown around the edges, about 8 minutes. Add
spinach and stir occasionally until the spinach is fully wilted.

2. Transfer spinach mixture to a sieve set over a bowl, and allow
it to drain until completely cooled. Press on the spinach with a
wooden spoon to extract as much liquid as possible. Transfer
spinach to two layers of paper towels, pull paper towels up
around the spinach, and gently squeeze out any liquid that
remains.

3. Place spinach mixture in a bowl with nutmeg, cayenne, and
feta. Add a pinch of kosher salt and pepper. Taste for seasoning.
When the taste is to your liking, gently stir in egg and lemon
juice.

4. Unroll phyllo dough and use a sharp knife to cut the stacks of
sheets into 5-inch squares. Cover with a clean, slightly damp
kitchen towel. Place a square on a clean work surface, and
brush with melted butter. Place another square on top, and
brush with more butter. Repeat until you create a rough stack
of 4–5 sheets. Spoon about 2 tablespoons of spinach mixture
onto the center of the stack of phyllo. Gather up the corners
of the phyllo sheets to enclose the filling, and tie with a strip
of leek. Place on a parchment paper–lined baking sheet, and
repeat to make the remaining purses. Refrigerate for 30
minutes.

5. Preheat oven to 425°F. Fold a large piece of aluminum foil like a
tent, and loosely cover the purses. Bake for 15 minutes, or until
the bottom of the purses start to turn golden brown. If they
are not brown after 15 minutes, remove the foil and bake for
5 minutes more. Remove from oven and allow purses to cool
completely. Best served at room temperature.

Leek and Cream Cheese Quiche

Once, while experimenting in the kitchen with omelets, I discovered how much I love cream cheese baked into eggs. It's heavenly. MAKES 10 MINI QUICHES

1. Preheat oven to 350°F. In the bowl of a food processor fitted with the steel blade attachment, pulse together flour, salt, and sugar. Add butter, and pulse until the mixture resembles coarse meal, but with some larger pieces of butter remaining.

2. Combine water and egg in a liquid measuring cup, and with the food processor on, slowly pour into the flour mixture. Pour dough onto a floured board and knead a few times to ensure everything is well combined. Wrap with plastic, and refrigerate for 20 minutes.

3. Roll dough out on a floured board, and cut into 10 4½-inch circles. Carefully fit each round into a standard muffin tin. Bake for 10–15 minutes, or until the edges just start to brown. Remove from oven, and allow to cool.

4. In a small skillet set over medium-low heat, sauté leeks in butter until tender, about 8 minutes. Spoon a small amount of leeks into the bottom of each crust, followed by a few dots of cream cheese.

5. In a medium bowl, whisk eggs with a pinch of salt and pepper. Pour egg mixture into crusts until nearly full to the top. Top each quiche with a sprinkling of cheddar cheese. Bake for 20–25 minutes, or until eggs are completely set.

For the crust:

2¼ cups unbleached all-purpose flour

1½ teaspoons kosher salt

2 teaspoons sugar

1 stick (8 tablespoons) cold unsalted butter, cut in pieces

5 tablespoons ice-cold water (ice removed)

1 egg, lightly beaten

For the filling:

1 leek, washed and cut into ½-inch pieces

2 teaspoons butter or olive oil

2 ounces cream cheese

6 large eggs

Kosher salt and pepper

½ cup shredded cheddar cheese

Buttermilk Panna Cotta with Blackberries

Panna cotta is an easy dessert that sounds very refined. I love to make it when the weather is warm and I have access to berries.

This recipe makes a little over 3 cups of panna cotta mixture, so the number of vessels you fill will depend on their size. I usually keep a couple of extra ramekins and custard cups at the ready so nothing goes to waste. SERVES 6-8

2 teaspoons unflavored gelatin (a little more than half a packet)

1 cup buttermilk

1 cup milk

1 cup heavy cream

2 teaspoons lemon zest

½ cup sugar

Pinch of kosher salt

1 teaspoon pure vanilla extract

1 cup blackberries

1. In a small bowl, whisk together gelatin and buttermilk. Set aside.

2. In a medium saucepan set over medium heat, combine milk, cream, lemon zest, sugar, and salt. Heat until nearly boiling. Remove from heat, and whisk in the buttermilk mixture and vanilla. Strain through a sieve and pour into small individual cups. Refrigerate for 4–6 hours, or overnight.

3. Sprinkle a small handful of blackberries on the top of each container of panna cotta, and serve.

Brown Sugar Amaretti

Ages ago, Martha Stewart hosted a cookie recipe contest on Martha Stewart Living. *One of the winning recipes was for Bonnie's Amaretti, They quickly became a family favorite. These Brown Sugar Amaretti are a variation on Bonnie's cookies.* MAKES ABOUT 20 SMALL COOKIES

1. In the bowl of a food processor fitted with the steel blade attachment, pulse almonds until finely ground. Add brown sugar and almond extract, and pulse a few more times until well combined.

2. In a medium stainless steel or glass bowl (a plastic bowl can prevent eggs from whipping), beat egg white until stiff peaks form. Add the almond mixture to the egg white, and fold until well combined.

3. Line a baking sheet with parchment paper or a silicone baking mat. Scoop dough by heaping teaspoonfuls (or use a 2-teaspoon-size cookie scoop) onto the parchment paper, about 1 inch apart. Let air-dry for 1 hour, or until only slightly sticky to the touch.

4. Preheat oven to 300°F. Bake cookies until edges almost start to brown, about 18–20 minutes. Dust with powdered sugar and let cool completely on baking sheet. Store in an airtight container for up to 3 days.

1 cup raw almonds

6 tablespoons brown sugar

½ teaspoon pure almond extract

1 egg white

1 tablespoon powdered sugar, for dusting

books to inspire:

Peter Pan, by J. M. Barrie
Spiderwick Chronicles, by Tony Diterlizzi and Holly Black
Sergei Prokofiev's Peter and the Wolf, adapted by Janet Schulman and illustrated by Peter Malone
Bambi: A Life in the Woods, by Felix Salten

french cafe

I speak French. Or I did, anyway. For about sixteen months, I left college and moved to Canada to work as a service missionary for my church, and lived in different cities all over Québec. My French was by no means eloquent, but I managed, and by the end of my stay in Canada, I was decently fluent. After I returned home, though, my handle on the language slipped very quickly from the lack of practice, and my tepid attempts at keeping it alive haven't fared well. I've been trying to read *Le Compte de Monte Cristo* for about six years now. I'm still on page 107.

It's sweet that my children hound me to teach them French now. Of course, I kick myself for not speaking it to them when they were babies. They would have learned it naturally, and I wouldn't have forgotten it. I suppose it's never too late, though, and the first word I've taught them is *crêpes*.

Our French Cafe party kicked off our language study by focusing on all things French. We borrowed an elegant French table from a friend and set it outside the front door. Then we broadcast some French accordion music on the iPod. To add to the fun, we played restaurant. My daughter was in charge of the menus, and the boys and I got to work in the kitchen. We prepped all of the toppings for the tartines and crêpes, and laid them out on the kitchen table so it would be easy enough even for my youngest to assemble the food once it was his turn to play waiter. I taught the kids simple phrases they might use at a restaurant in France, and they practiced while we ate our food and sipped our lemonade sodas

For your party, you can create a French cafe like we did, set up a typical Italian restaurant (like the one the twins re-created for their parents in the 1960s *The Parent Trap*), or design a Chinese takeout establishment complete with fold-up boxes and disposable chopsticks.

RECIPES:
Assorted Tartines
Strawberry Crêpes
Lemonade Sodas

Assorted Tartines

Tartines are open-faced sandwiches from France. Since you can top them with virtually anything, they were perfect for our French Cafe party. Though the bread is toasted first and then topped with something cool, we couldn't resist re-toasting some of ours with the delicious toppings we had on hand. They were like eating deconstructed—or rather, reconstructed—cheese fondue. MAKES ABOUT 8 TARTINES

1 loaf round bread, very thinly sliced and lightly toasted

Assorted toppings:

Meats, such as cooked chicken, smoked salmon, or shaved ham

Fruits, such as thinly sliced Granny Smith apples and Bartlett pears

Vegetables, such as roasted red peppers, cucumbers, sprouts, arugula, or other greens

Caramelized Onion Jam (recipe follows)

Goat Cheese Spread (recipe follows)

Cheeses, such as Gorgonzola, Fontina, Havarti, or brie

Sea salt and pepper

For cold tartines:

1. Place desired combination of toppings on toast, slice in wedges, and serve.

Our favorite cold combination:

Goat Cheese Spread (recipe below), topped with smoked salmon, cucumbers, and sprouts, and sprinkled with sea salt

For toasted tartines:

1. Preheat oven to 425°F. Assemble your tartines as you like, starting with a piece of toast, layering it with meat and vegetables or fruit, and topping it with cheese.

2. Place tartines on a baking sheet, and toast in the oven for 5–10 minutes, or until the cheese is melted. Slice in wedges and serve.

Our favorite toasted combinations:

Brie, Granny Smith apple slices, and shaved ham

Havarti, Bartlett pears, Caramelized Onion Jam (recipe below), and a sprinkling of Gorgonzola

books to inspire:

Madeline, by Ludwig Bemelmans
The Adventures of Tintin, by Hergé
Le Petit Prince, by Antoine de Saint-Exupéry
Anatole, by Eve Titus, illustrated by Paul Galdone

Caramelized Onion Jam

Caramelizing onions is quite time-consuming, which is why I like to make a big batch and refrigerate them, so I'll have some whenever needed. These will keep for up to two weeks. MAKES APPROXIMATELY 1 CUP

3 tablespoons unsalted butter

4–5 medium yellow onions, thinly sliced

Kosher salt

1 teaspoon balsamic vinegar

1. In a large heavy-bottomed pot, melt butter over low heat. Add onions and stir until coated in butter. Add a generous pinch of salt. Cook, stirring often, until onions are tender and translucent, about 10 minutes.

2. Raise the heat to medium. Let onions cook down until a thin film of browned onion coats some of the bottom of the pot. Pour in about 1 tablespoon of water, and stir to incorporate the brown color. Keep repeating this process until the onions reach the shade of caramel brown you are looking for. This process can take up to 30 minutes. Stir in balsamic vinegar, and add more salt to taste.

Goat Cheese Spread

MAKES ENOUGH FOR 8 TARTINES

6 ounces goat cheese (chèvre), at room temperature

3 tablespoons mayonnaise or Vegenaise

2 teaspoons dried dill weed

1 tablespoon finely chopped fresh chives

Pinch of kosher salt

Combine ingredients evenly in a small bowl.

music to set the scene:

Gus Viseur Les Archives de L'Accordéon, Marianne Melodie, 2010

French Accordion Music, Master Classics Records, 2009

Café de Paris: Echoes of France, Volume 4, Blue Orchid, 2009

Strawberry Crêpes

The first crêpe almost always turns out too buttery to serve. It becomes the treat for the cook or whoever is passing through the kitchen. I always sprinkle mine with a little bit of powdered sugar. MAKES 10–15 CRÊPES

1 pound strawberries, washed, hulled, and sliced

1 teaspoon balsamic vinegar

2 tablespoons granulated sugar

1 cup all-purpose flour

¼ teaspoon kosher salt

1 cup milk, plus up to 1 cup more for controlling consistency

2 eggs

2 tablespoons unsalted butter, melted, plus more for pan

Whipped Cream (recipe follows)

Powdered sugar, for dusting

1. In a small bowl, stir together strawberries, balsamic vinegar, and 1 tablespoon sugar. Set aside.

2. In a large bowl, combine flour, salt, and remaining tablespoon of sugar. Make a well in the center. In a small bowl, combine milk and eggs. Pour a small amount into the well, and whisk slowly to incorporate into the flour. Keep adding more of the liquid ingredients until both mixtures come together in a smooth batter. Cover and refrigerate for at least 30 minutes to rest. Batter should be thin, like whipping cream. Add more milk, a couple tablespoons at a time, to achieve this consistency.

3. Set a large nonstick frying pan over medium heat, and brush with a small amount of melted butter. Ladle in about ¼–⅓ cup of batter, swirling the pan until the entire bottom surface is covered in a thin film of batter. Cook until the batter appears dry and spongy on top, and the edges begin to brown. Carefully lift the crêpe on one edge, and run spatula around the perimeter of the crêpe to separate it from the pan. Slide the spatula fully under the crêpe and flip. Allow to cook for about 30 seconds more, and transfer to a plate. The next several crêpes should not need additional butter in the pan, but add more as necessary. Cook as many as you need; batter can be stored in the refrigerator for up to 24 hours. Add enough milk at each use to achieve the creamy consistency.

4. Fill each crêpe with strawberries and whipped cream, dust with powdered sugar, and top with a dollop of cream and strawberry slices.

½ cup heavy cream

2 tablespoons powdered sugar

½ teaspoon pure vanilla extract

½ teaspoon pure almond extract

Whipped Cream

Place all the ingredients in a bowl, and beat them together with an electric mixer until stiff peaks form. Do not overbeat.

Let the kids dream up other ingredients for the crêpes, such as blackberries, peaches, brie, or raspberries. Have them design a dessert menu to display the choices.

Lemonade Sodas

Fizzy lemonade is such a French thing, n'est-ce pas? I thought it would be perfect for our cafe. MAKES 6 8-OUNCE BOTTLES

1 cup water

1 cup superfine sugar

1 cup freshly squeezed lemon juice (about 6–8 lemons)

1½ liters seltzer or sparkling water

1. In a medium saucepan, combine water and sugar, and set over medium-high heat. Bring to a boil, and let cook for 1 minute. Remove from heat, and let cool completely.

2. Combine lemon juice with the sugar syrup in a pitcher. Slowly pour in 1 liter of the seltzer. Taste for flavor. Add more seltzer as desired. Use a funnel to pour into individual bottles.

variations on a theme:

Bring the party indoors and make it into a fancy restaurant, complete with classical music, candles, and a three-course meal.

summer

garden tea party

My fascination with all things English began as a young woman when my friend gave me my first issue of *Victoria* magazine. I would pore over it for hours, wishing I could be in those photographs—to sit in the lush green gardens with their bowers of roses and borders of lavender. Each picture was dewy and romantic, like a John Singer Sargent painting.

Some of the most beautiful articles in *Victoria* I can remember featured garden picnics or sumptuous tea parties. The food was always gorgeous—scones and tea sandwiches, sugared flowers, or tarts covered in berries.

Though we're not tea drinkers in our family—herbal tea or lemonade is more our style—I love trying to re-create the magic of those tea parties. They are the perfect way to gather the family together for a small, intimate celebration.

For our Garden Tea Party, I found a spot at a park near our home that had a bench and cobblestone walkways. Everyone dressed up, donned their best manners, and off we went. Since the weather was warm and we had no means to heat a kettle, we brought iced herbal tea. It was the perfect complement to our tea sandwiches and scones.

The beauty of a tea party is that everyone can enjoy it. Since it's not a major meal, if my daughter wants to skip the sandwiches because they don't resemble candy, I'm okay with that. Teatime food is open to interpretation, and that takes the pressure off everyone.

Celebrate your own tea party somewhere lovely. It could be at your dining room table, in the backyard, or even at a park. Use the time to talk about books you are reading, individually and as a family. Encourage children to leave arguments and complaints at the door and focus on positive conversation.

RECIPES:
Cucumber and Sprouts Tea Sandwiches
Egg Salad and Avocado Tea Sandwiches
Vanilla Bean Cream Scones
Raspberry Lemon Curd
Herbal Iced Tea

Cucumber and Sprouts Tea Sandwiches

In my American brain, no tea party is complete without cucumber sandwiches. I made these with German pumpernickel I found at the local grocery store, but any brown bread will do. MAKES 16 SMALL TEA SANDWICHES

¼ cup sour cream

2 ounces cream cheese

2 teaspoons lime juice

Pinch of kosher salt

1 teaspoon dill weed

1 tablespoon freshly chopped
   parsley

8 slices thinly sliced
   pumpernickel bread

1 English cucumber, very thinly
   sliced

Handful of radish or alfalfa
   sprouts

1. In a small bowl, combine sour cream, cream cheese, lime juice, salt, and herbs. Spread on 8 slices of bread. Top 4 of the slices with cucumbers and sprouts. Press the remaining 4 slices of bread, spread side down, on top of the cucumbers and sprouts.

2. Wrap sandwiches with plastic wrap and refrigerate for 2 hours or overnight. With a very sharp knife, remove crusts and slice into triangular wedges.

Egg Salad and Avocado Tea Sandwiches

Not too long ago, I discovered the delights of pairing ripe avocado with egg salad. Though similar in texture, they form the perfect complement. MAKES 16 SMALL TEA SANDWICHES

1. In a medium bowl, combine eggs, mayonnaise, mustard, pickles, and salt.

2. Spread egg mixture onto 4 slices of bread, and top with avocado slices. Spread the other 4 slices of bread with the butter, and press onto the avocado. Wrap with plastic and refrigerate for 20 minutes. Remove plastic, and with a very sharp knife, cut off crusts and slice each sandwich into 4 long rectangles.

6 hard-boiled eggs, roughly chopped

⅓ cup mayonnaise or Vegenaise

1 tablespoon coarse mustard

4 mini sweet pickles, finely chopped

Pinch of kosher salt

8 slices thinly sliced sourdough bread

1 avocado, thinly sliced

2 tablespoons salted butter, at room temperature

get creative:

Encourage everyone to practice his or her best manners, and make a game of it. Anytime someone makes a faux pas, the person to correct them must use their very best posh accent: "Chahhlie, dahling, would you kindly take your elbows off the table?"

Vanilla Bean Cream Scones

Adding vanilla bean to both the dough and the sugar on top, takes these simple scones to a whole new level. If you can't find vanilla beans, or you find the price inhibitive, you can simply leave them out, and the scones will still be delicious. No worries. MAKES 8 SCONES

1 vanilla bean

⅓ cup sugar, plus 2 tablespoons

2 cups unbleached all-purpose flour, plus more for rolling

2½ teaspoons baking powder

¾ teaspoon salt

4 tablespoons cold unsalted butter, cut into pieces

1 cup heavy cream, plus 1 tablespoon

1 egg, lightly beaten

1 teaspoon pure vanilla extract

1. Preheat oven to 400°F. Line a large baking sheet with parchment paper.

2. Cut the vanilla bean in half. Slice each half the long way, and scrape the seeds. Put the seeds from one half into a large bowl, and scrape the seeds from the other half into a small bowl.

3. In the large bowl with the vanilla bean seeds, add ⅓ cup sugar, flour, baking powder, and salt. Whisk to combine. Add butter pieces, toss to coat, and then, using a pastry cutter or your hands, cut the butter into the flour mixture until it resembles coarse meal.

4. In a separate bowl, combine 1 cup cream, egg, and vanilla extract. Pour into flour mixture, and stir until just combined.

5. Dust a board or countertop well with flour. While handling it as little as possible, place the dough on the flour and pat down to 1 inch thick. Use a 2½-inch cookie cutter to cut the dough into circles. Place scones on the prepared baking sheet about 2 inches apart.

6. Mix reserved vanilla bean scrapings with remaining sugar, using a fork or your hands to make sure it is fully incorporated. Pass through a sieve, if desired, to remove vanilla bean fibers.

7. Brush tops of scones with heavy cream, and sprinkle with vanilla sugar. Bake for 12–15 minutes, or until just barely golden brown around the bottom edges.

variations on a theme:

If you don't have a garden to host the party, pick a local park or prepare a deck or rooftop with potted plants.

Raspberry Lemon Curd

A few years ago, I posted a recipe for Raspberry Lemonade Bars on my blog, which ended up being a big hit. This Raspberry Lemon Curd is nearly the same thing, minus the cookie. It's faster to make, and you can eat it with a spoon. MAKES 1½ CUPS

1 cup frozen raspberries, defrosted (after they're defrosted, they look like about ¼ cup)

Zest of 2 lemons

5 tablespoons unsalted butter

1 cup granulated sugar

3 large eggs

⅓ cup lemon juice (from about 2 lemons)

Pinch of salt

1. Press raspberries through a fine sieve to extract all the pulp. Set aside.

2. In a medium bowl, cream together zest, butter, and sugar with the back of a wooden spoon. Incorporate eggs one at a time, and mix until smooth. Add raspberry pulp, lemon juice, and salt. The mixture will be curdled.

3. Pour mixture into a medium saucepan and cook over low heat, stirring constantly, for about 10–12 minutes, or until it is thick enough to coat the back of a wooden spoon. Strain through a fine sieve into a bowl and cool completely. Keep in the refrigerator or freezer until ready to serve.

books to inspire:
The Secret Garden, by Frances Hodgson Burnett
Linnea in Monet's Garden, by Cristina Bjork, Lena Anderson, and Joan Sandin
Tom's Midnight Garden, by Philippa Pearce
Alice's Adventures in Wonderland, by Lewis Carroll

Herbal Iced Tea

This iced tea is half herbal tea, half juice—a perfect way for different preferences to meet in the middle.
SERVES 4

1. Pour boiling water over tea bags. Let steep for 2 minutes, then remove tea bags.

2. Place cold water and fruit juice in a pitcher or carafe. Slowly pour in hot herbal tea. Stir in ice and sliced lemon.

1 cup boiling water

4 bags fruit-flavored herbal tea, such as Lemon Zinger from Celestial Seasonings

1 cup cold water

1 cup 100% fruit juice, such as white grape, apple, or cranberry

2 cups ice

1 lemon, thinly sliced

music to set the scene:

Violin Concerto no. 1, by Johann Sebastian Bach
Concerto for Guitar, Strings, and B.c. in D Major: I. Allegro, by Antonio Vivaldi
Concerto a 5 in B Flat, op. 9, no. 1 for Violin, Strings, and Continuo, by Tomaso Albinoni

last day
of school
backyard
pizza party

When I was a girl, my summer vacation didn't start until the very last week of June. We would spend those final days in a muggy classroom, legs sticking to our chairs, fanning ourselves with accordion-folded paper salvaged from the recycling bin. We never had any work left to do, so the teachers were just as bored as we were, watching the minutes drag by until we fulfilled our 180-day requirement for the year. A few times my elementary school principal set up a projector in the cafeteria so we could watch Charlie Chaplin movies and *The Three Stooges* in an endless stream.

But then, just at the moment when we might have lost the will to live, the bell would ring, and summer vacation would begin. Within moments of exiting the school, I would start to panic. I would be walking right back through those doors before I knew it if I didn't make the most of every summer moment. That last day of school wasn't time to go home and be bored, or watch TV—it was time to party.

To kick off my kids' summer vacation, they invited a few of their friends to our Backyard Pizza Party, knowing summer has a way of sweeping classmates away—returning them only when school begins again. When the guests arrived, my son showed the kids how to get their pizzas ready for grilling, and my daughter directed a treasure hunt for a small chest containing fixings for s'mores. While they searched for the

RECIPES:
Grilled Pizza
Ultimate Homemade S'mores

get creative:

Plan a treasure hunt. Fill a wooden trunk with everything the kids will need to make the Ultimate Homemade S'mores: a jar of Milk Chocolate Truffle Sauce, Honey Flavored Marshmallows, and Homemade Graham Crackers. Have a child design the map and hide the treasure. When the treasure is found, start up the fire and make the s'mores.

treasure, we listened to Ralph Vaughan Williams's *English Folk Song Suite* to get them into a swashbuckling mood. Although our book inspiration was *Treasure Island,* we didn't do much reading for the party. We were on vacation, after all.

This party is for grasping those first few moments of summer before they slip away too quickly. Yours does not need to be as elaborate as ours, especially when you invite a group of friends. Depending on the amount of time and resources you have, you can fire up the grill and make homemade marshmallows for roasting, as we did. For a quicker approach, you can simply order pizza and roast store-bought marshmallows.

music to set the scene:

English Folk Song Suite, by Ralph Vaughan Williams
Soundtrack from *Pirates of the Caribbean: The Curse of the Black Pearl,* by Klaus Badelt
Soundtrack from *Pirates of the Caribbean: At World's End,* by Hans Zimmer

Grilled Pizza

This is a great way to enjoy homemade pizza when it's too hot to cook in the house. MAKES 8 PERSONAL PIZZAS

3½ cups bread flour

1 tablespoon instant yeast

2 tablespoons extra-virgin olive oil

1½ teaspoons kosher salt

1¼ cups warm water (110°F), plus more if needed

1 stick (8 tablespoons) salted butter, melted

2 cloves garlic, finely grated or pressed through a garlic press

Tomato Sauce (recipe follows)

Assorted toppings, such as mozzarella cheese, basil, mushrooms, peppers, and pepperoni

1. In the bowl of an electric mixer fitted with the dough hook, combine flour, yeast, olive oil, and salt. Slowly pour in the water. If dough appears to be dry, add more water—up to 2 tablespoons—to make a stiff but workable dough. Knead on low speed for 10 minutes. Place in an oiled bowl, cover with plastic or a kitchen towel, and let rise for 45 minutes, or until doubled in bulk.

2. Preheat the grill. Divide dough into 8 equal pieces. Roll out each piece, and place on a floured piece of parchment paper laid on a baking sheet.

3. Mix melted butter and garlic, and brush each piece of dough with the mixture. Place on the grill, butter side down, and cook until the top starts to bubble and grill marks appear on the bottom. Return crusts to the floured piece of parchment paper, brush the uncooked side with more of the garlic butter, and turn over so the grill markings face up.

4. Use a large spoon or ladle to spread tomato sauce on the crusts, then arrange desired toppings on top. Return to the grill, cover the grill, and cook until cheese is melted and toppings are cooked. Cooking time will vary with each grill.

Tomato Sauce

1. In a large skillet, heat olive oil over medium heat. Add garlic, red pepper flakes, and rosemary. Cook for about 1 minute, until fragrant.

2. Place tomatoes in a blender and pulse a few times to make a puree. Pour into the skillet, reduce to medium-low heat, and simmer, uncovered, for 15 minutes. Season with salt and pepper.

1 tablespoon extra-virgin olive oil

2 cloves garlic, finely chopped

Pinch of red pepper flakes

2 teaspoons finely chopped fresh rosemary, or 1 teaspoon dried

1 (28-ounce) can diced or whole tomatoes

Salt and pepper, to taste

Ultimate Homemade S'mores

What kid isn't happy with s'mores, whether made with store-bought ingredients or otherwise? But if you go the extra mile, and make these Ultimate S'mores, you'll be everyone's favorite person, I promise.
MAKES 10

1. Spread Chocolate Truffle Sauce on a Homemade Graham Cracker. Spear a marshmallow with a stick if roasting in an open fire,* or a skewer if roasting over a hot stove burner. Turn slowly, about 1-3 inches away from the flame. Roast until golden brown.

2. Place the marshmallow on top of the Truffle Sauce, place another Graham Cracker over the roasted marshmallow. Gently squeeze the two crackers together and slide out the stick or skewer. Enjoy immediately. Repeat with remaining crackers and marshmallows.

Homemade Graham Crackers (recipe follows)

Honey-Flavored Marshmallows (recipe follows)

Chocolate Truffle Sauce (recipe follows)

---

*Always use the greatest care when cooking over an open flame. Adult supervision is imperative.

---

books to inspire:

Treasure Island, by Robert Louis Stevenson
How I Became a Pirate, by Melinda Long
The Count of Monte Cristo, by Alexandre Dumas

Homemade Graham Crackers

For years I searched for a good homemade graham cracker recipe to go with my homemade marshmallows. Getting ideas from both Martha Stewart and bloggers on the Web, I came up with this one. These graham crackers are a little sturdier than your average store-bought variety, and tastier—perfect for out-of-this-world s'mores.

MAKES ABOUT 20 CRACKERS

2 cups whole-wheat pastry flour (available at health food stores)

½ teaspoon baking powder

½ teaspoon kosher salt

5 tablespoons unsalted butter, at room temperature

½ cup brown sugar

3 tablespoons honey

1 tablespoon molasses

2 tablespoons milk

1 teaspoon pure vanilla extract

1. In a small bowl, whisk together flour, baking powder, and salt. Set aside.

2. In the bowl of an electric mixer fitted with the paddle attachment, cream together butter and brown sugar until light and fluffy, about 2 minutes. Add honey and molasses, and mix until well incorporated. Beat in milk and vanilla.

3. With the mixer on low, slowly add the dry ingredients, and mix until dough becomes well incorporated. Turn dough out onto a well-floured board, and knead a few times to ensure good distribution of ingredients. Wrap in plastic wrap, and refrigerate for 30 minutes to 1 hour.

4. Roll out dough between 2 sheets of plastic wrap or on a well-floured board until it is ⅛ inch thick. With the plastic still on, transfer rolled-out dough to baking sheets, and place in freezer for 20 minutes.

5. Preheat oven to 350°F. Line a baking sheet with a nonstick silicone baking pad such as a Silpat, or with a piece of parchment paper.

6. Peel back the plastic, and with a pizza cutter or a fluted pastry wheel, cut dough into 3-inch squares. Place squares ½ inch apart on the baking sheet. Use the blunt edge of a skewer to dot dough with holes. (If at any time the dough gets too soft to work with, place on a cookie sheet and return to the freezer for a few minutes.) Bake for 8–10 minutes, or until edges just barely start to brown. Allow to cool in the pan for 10 minutes, then remove to a wire rack to cool completely. These will keep, uncovered, for 2 days.

Honey-Flavored Marshmallows

These have a hint of honey flavor and are wonderful toasted or plain. Making marshmallows is a sticky, messy process, but everything will wash off easily with water once you're done. MAKES 16 HUGE MARSHMALLOWS

1. Dust the bottom of an 8 x 8-inch square pan with 1 cup powdered sugar; reserve the rest for later. In the bowl of an electric mixer fitted with the whisk attachment, dissolve the gelatin in ¾ cup water.

2. In a medium saucepan, combine ½ cup water, granulated sugar, salt, and honey. Set over medium heat, and stir frequently until the mixture starts to boil. Once it begins to boil, stop stirring and wait for the temperature to reach 238°F (soft ball stage) on a candy thermometer. If you don't have a thermometer, watch the syrup carefully. At first, the bubbles will come very high up the sides of the pan. As the temperature of the syrup rises, the bubbles will start to relax. Once they do, check the candy by spooning out a small amount of the syrup and dropping it into cool water. If you can hold the syrup in your hands and shape it into a soft blob, then it's ready.

3. With the mixer on low, slowly pour the honey syrup into the dissolved gelatin. Raise the speed to medium, and then to high. Add the vanilla, and whisk for 5–7 minutes, or until thick, foamy, and white. Pour into the prepared pan with the help of a silicone spatula. If the mixture is unwieldy, use wet fingers to smooth it down. Sprinkle with ½ cup powdered sugar, and allow to dry overnight.

4. Use a wet knife to separate the marshmallow from the edges of the pan. Pull out the marshmallow, and use kitchen shears or a wet knife to cut into squares. Roll each square in the last ½ cup of powdered sugar, and tap off the excess.

2 cups powdered sugar

4 packages unflavored gelatin

1¼ cups cool water

3 cups granulated cane sugar

½ teaspoon kosher salt

½ cup honey

2 teaspoons pure vanilla extract

Chocolate Truffle Sauce

This milk chocolate sauce is perfect for spreading on graham crackers for gourmet s'mores. This is a bit thicker than the Two-Minute Ganache (page 162), but either recipe could be used. MAKES 2 CUPS

½ cup heavy cream

1 teaspoon pure vanilla extract

1½ cups good-quality milk chocolate chips (I use the Guittard brand)

½ cup semisweet chocolate chips

1. In a large microwave-safe bowl, heat cream on high until boiling, about 1 minute. Pour in vanilla and chocolate chips, and allow to sit for 2 minutes.

2. Whisk chocolate and cream until smooth. If any chocolate remains unmelted, microwave mixture on high for 20 seconds at a time, whisking well after each interval, until smooth and melted. Pour into jars and refrigerate, if desired.

variations on a theme:

Instead of a pizza party, make it an ice cream sundae party. Provide the ice cream and cones, and ask each guest to bring his or her favorite topping.

walk on the beach

When I was around ten years old, a few of my neighborhood friends had pools in their backyards, and my pool-less friends and I would come up with long lists of why pools were better than the ocean: They were warmer, less sandy, less salty, and free of sharks and jellyfish. As valid as our arguments were in our small world, we couldn't comprehend how lucky we were to live so close to a beach—less than a ten-minute drive. We had nothing to compare it to, other than the fortunes of our pool-owning neighbors.

As I grew older, I started to appreciate the beauty of living by the ocean. I learned that a swim in the icy Atlantic was the perfect remedy to a hot and muggy day. I loved going there with friends, or taking long walks with my mom as the sun set. Sometimes, my mother would hear of a great beach on Cape Cod, and we'd venture the long drive to search for it. We'd spend hours on the quiet shores, uncrowded by tourists, looking for sea glass and perfectly sun-bleached clamshells.

Between trips back East, my kids tell me how much they miss the ocean. I guess they haven't spent enough time around the sea to take it for granted like I did. Living inland has some advantages.

For our little party on the beach, I kept thinking of *Prince Caspian* by C. S. Lewis. When the four Pevensie children discover themselves in Narnia, they spend much of their first day exploring the beach near Cair Paravel. Only Edmund manages to carry his effects with him to Narnia, and his lunch of two sandwiches is the only food they have to share among the four of them. Eventually, they find an orchard of apple trees, which they had planted when they had reined as kings and queens there in *The Lion, the Witch and the Wardrobe*.

To picnic on the beach, we brought our food in individual wooden baskets. We don't live on the coast, so we found a small

beach on a reservoir near our home. The kids enjoyed them-selves by skipping rocks and walking along the small shore.

When you have your celebration at the beach, you can take a walk in the evening (like we did) or make it a more tra-ditional beach trip and visit on a hot, sunny day. Try to do all your activities together instead of splitting up. Swim together, read together under a sun umbrella, or comb tidal pools for sea life together.

variations on a theme:

If you don't have access to a beach, try taking a walk on a mountain path or in a large public park, and bring along a picnic.

Chicken Salad Sandwiches

Tarragon is a mild, leafy herb that pairs well with chicken, so I added it to this salad. If for some reason you can't find it, just add a pinch more dill. MAKES 6 SANDWICHES

1. Cover the raisins with water in a microwavable container, and microwave on high for 45 seconds. Set aside.

2. In a large bowl, whisk together mayonnaise, vinegar, honey, salt, herbs, and cayenne pepper. Drain raisins and add to the bowl, along with the almonds and chicken. Stir to combine. Spoon onto sandwich rolls.

½ cup raisins

½ cup mayonnaise

2 tablespoons rice vinegar

1 tablespoon honey

½ teaspoon kosher salt

2 tablespoons chopped fresh tarragon

½ teaspoon dried dill weed

Pinch of cayenne pepper

2 tablespoons sliced almonds

4 cooked chicken breasts, cut into ¼-inch cubes

6 sandwich rolls, sliced in half

music to set the scene:

Water Music, by George Frideric Handel
Four Sea Interludes for Peter Grimes, by Benjamin Britten
"And God Created Great Whales," op. 229, no. 1, by Alan Hovhannes
"Water Night," by Eric Whitacre

Corkscrew Pasta Salad

Isn't pasta salad fun? You start with whatever vegetables you have on hand, and just when you think it's going to be too healthy to really enjoy, you douse it with a good helping of vinaigrette and pile on curlicues of pure white carbohydrate bliss. Perfect picnic food. SERVES 6

1. Cook pasta until it is al dente. Drain and rinse with cool water.

2. Toss with all the other ingredients in a large bowl. Serve chilled or at room temperature.

½ pound pasta, such as fusilli bucati or another favorite pasta shape

½ English cucumber, cut into ½-inch pieces

1 cup cherry or grape tomatoes, cut in halves

2 cups broccoli florets, cut into bite-size pieces

3 ounces feta cheese, crumbled

8–10 large basil leaves, rolled and cut into thin slices

Balsamic Vinaigrette (recipe follows)

Balsamic Vinaigrette

Whisk together all the ingredients, and taste for proper seasoning.

3 tablespoons balsamic vinegar

3 tablespoons very good olive oil

1 tablespoon Dijon mustard

1 tablespoon pure maple syrup

2–3 chives, finely chopped

Pinch of kosher salt and black pepper

get creative:

If you're able to take a walk on an ocean beach, collect seashells that can later be used as decorations around the house or for picture frames to commemorate the event.

Apple Dumplings

These apple dumplings were inspired by the line in Prince Caspian *when C. S. Lewis mentions roasted apples aren't very good without sugar. These have plenty of sugar—and butter, for good measure.* MAKES 6 DUMPLINGS

For the pastry:

2¼ cups unbleached all-purpose flour

¼ cup sugar

1 teaspoon salt

2 sticks (16 tablespoons) cold unsalted butter, cut into small pieces

6 tablespoons ice-cold water

For the rest:

2 tablespoons unbleached all-purpose flour

2 tablespoons almond flour

⅓ cup brown sugar

½ cup quick oats

Pinch of salt

½ teaspoon cinnamon

¼ teaspoon ground nutmeg

1 tablespoon orange zest

4 tablespoons cool unsalted butter

6 small Granny Smith apples

2 tablespoons heavy cream

¼ cup sanding sugar or granulated sugar

1. To make the pastry, combine flour, sugar, and salt in a food processor fitted with the steel blade, and pulse once or twice. Add butter to the flour mixture. Pulse a few times until it resembles coarse meal, but some of the larger pieces of butter remain. Add the water, a little at a time, and pulse until the dough almost comes together. Pour out onto a lightly floured board, and gently knead the dough a time or two to ensure everything comes together. Divide the dough in half, and wrap each half in plastic wrap. Refrigerate at least 20 minutes.

2. For the filling, combine the flours, brown sugar, quick oats, salt, spices, and orange zest in the bowl of an electric mixer fitted with the paddle attachment (or in the food processor again). With the mixer on low, add the butter and mix until all ingredients come together.

3. Preheat oven to 400°F. Line a baking sheet with parchment paper. Remove the dough from the refrigerator and cut each ball in fourths. Roll a piece of dough out to make an 8-inch circle. Peel and core the apples. Stuff the middle of an apple with as much filling as will fit. Place in the center of the circle of dough, and pull the dough up the sides of the apple, using water to make the dough stick and seal in the apple. Repeat with the remainder of the apples, and place on the prepared baking sheet.

4. On a lightly floured board, roll the remaining dough to a ¼-inch thickness. Use a cookie cutter, such as a medium-size star shape, to cut dough into 6 shapes. Use a little bit of water to press the shape onto the top of each apple. Brush with cream, and sprinkle with sanding sugar.

5. Bake for 35–40 minutes, or until tops are golden brown. Serve warm or at room temperature.

Minty Limeade

A friend once gave me a slushy made from all the same ingredients, and it was the most refreshing drink I'd ever had. Since the ice wouldn't last very long at the beach, I adapted the recipe to a simple drink.
SERVES 4–6

Combine juices and mint, and pour over crushed ice in individual glasses.

Juice of 6–8 limes, about ⅓–½ cup

3 cups white grape juice

10–12 fresh mint leaves, bruised

2 cups crushed ice

books to inspire:
The Chronicles of Narnia, by C. S. Lewis
The Cay, by Theodore Taylor
The Little Island, by Margaret Wise Brown
Time of Wonder, by Robert McCloskey

concert on the green

Many of my childhood memories are of concerts on the town green or at another public park. My mom was always finding one free concert or another to attend. We would help my parents lug folding chairs and blankets to an empty patch of grass, and pull out a small picnic of peanut butter and jelly sandwiches with a cooler full of water.

In high school, the cool thing to do was take the "T," Massachusetts's train system, into the city with friends to attend a Boston Pops concert at the Hatch Shell on the Boston Esplanade. We'd bring sweatshirts and blankets and squeeze together amongst the crowd to hear the orchestra play John Williams's compositions or "Stars and Stripes Forever."

My sister and her children now have the good fortune of living near Tanglewood, the summer home of the Boston Symphony Orchestra in Lenox, Massachusetts. All season long, the BSO performs outdoor concerts, and it's tradition for many people to bring full gourmet, candlelit dinners.

Of course, I miss the wealth of outdoor musical performances in Massachusetts, but concerts on the green are easy enough to find in nearly every community. With a little research on the Internet, we found several in our own area. Our party was somewhere between the peanut butter and jelly sandwiches and carrot sticks my mom packed for us and the candlelit dinners at Tanglewood.

I was inspired by the Anne of Green Gables series by Lucy Maude Montgomery. Anne is an orphan whose imagination, love of literature, and pursuit of education lead her through

RECIPES:
Fried Chicken Strips
Mukimame Succotash
Easy Buttermilk Biscuits
Raspberry Cordial
Plum Bars

music to set the scene:
Listen to whatever music is featured at the concert, along with other pieces by the same composer, or any CD the orchestra has produced.

an extraordinary life. While planning for our concert on the green, we paid mind to Anne's eagerness to delve into cultural experiences and how fine music enriches our lives. In respect to her, we made a kid-friendly Raspberry Cordial, certainly nothing a bosom friend would get drunk on. Before the concert, the children and I looked into what music would be performed and did some research on the composer. We sat on our blankets, enjoying our fried chicken and succotash. As we waited for the sun to go down and the performers to begin, we talked about the composer, his life, and his music.

To make this experience your own, you may choose to attend an outdoor play or even a storytelling festival instead of a concert. Read the play with the children before you go so they can follow along, or find out as much as you can about the actors. Don't hesitate to be creative with the kind of food you bring, or how you set it up. Call the venue ahead of time to find out if outside food is allowed on the grounds.

variations on a theme:

Attend an outdoor theatrical production, and read the play beforehand. Or, attend the symphony at their usual indoor venue, and enjoy your picnic and discussion before or after the concert.

Fried Chicken Strips

My daughter is one of the pickiest eaters I know, and she loves this recipe. SERVES 6

1½ pounds skinless chicken breast tenders

1½ cups buttermilk

¼ teaspoon cayenne pepper

2 cups all-purpose flour

2 teaspoons kosher salt

½ teaspoon freshly ground black pepper

1 teaspoon paprika

Enough corn oil or vegetable oil to fill your skillet with 1 inch of oil

1 stick (8 tablespoons) unsalted butter

1. Place chicken in a glass or other nonreactive bowl with buttermilk and cayenne pepper. Stir to coat the chicken completely. Cover with plastic and allow to marinate for 6–8 hours, or up to 24 hours.

2. In a shallow dish, combine flour, salt, pepper, and paprika. Dip each piece of chicken in the flour mixture, then back into the buttermilk, and then dip in the flour mixture again for a final coating. Set on a baking sheet until ready to fry.

3. Pour oil in a large cast-iron skillet, and set over medium-high heat. Add butter, and let melt. When butter has completely melted and starts to make the oil cloudy with bubbles, drop a small errant piece of the flour/buttermilk coating into the hot oil. If it rises to the surface within a few seconds, the oil is ready for frying.

4. Place about 4 pieces of chicken in the oil, and fry for about 5 minutes per side, until the chicken is cooked through and the coating is golden brown. Drain on paper towels. Repeat with remaining chicken pieces.

Mukimame Succotash

Succotash is traditionally made with lima beans. Unfortunately, lima beans are one of the few things I don't care for. Mukimame—edamame without their pods—turned out to be a perfect compromise.

SERVES 6

1. Heat oil in a large skillet set over medium-low heat. Add onions and sauté until nearly tender, about 8 minutes. Stir in bell pepper and cayenne, and cook until the pepper starts to soften, about 2 minutes more.

2. Stir in mukimame, corn, salt, and black pepper, and raise the heat to medium-high. Cook for 5–10 minutes more, stirring occasionally, until the corn and mukimame are cooked through and start to brown on the edges.

2 teaspoons extra virgin olive oil

1 medium yellow onion, finely diced

1 orange bell pepper, finely diced

Pinch of cayenne pepper

2 cups frozen mukimame

2 cups frozen corn kernels

½ teaspoon kosher salt

Pinch of freshly ground black pepper

books to inspire:

Anne of Green Gables series, by L. M. Montgomery
The Philharmonic Gets Dressed, by Karla Kuskin
Can You Hear It? by William Lach

Easy Buttermilk Biscuits

These are the easiest biscuits I have ever made. You don't need a mixer, and they take less than five minutes to throw together. They're perfect for teaching someone their first lesson in baking. MAKES 16 BISCUITS

2 cups flour, plus about ¼ cup more for rolling

1½ teaspoons baking powder

¼ teaspoon baking soda

¾ teaspoon kosher salt

1 stick (8 tablespoons) butter, cold but not frozen

¾ cup buttermilk

¼ cup heavy cream, plus more for brushing

1. Preheat oven to 450°F. Place 2 cups flour in a large bowl, and whisk in baking powder, baking soda, and salt. Add butter, and use your hands to rub the butter into small pieces and disperse throughout the flour mixture. When the mixture looks rough and butter is the size of corn flakes, stir in buttermilk and cream. The mixture will be very sticky.

2. Pour ¼ cup flour onto a board, and dump dough onto the flour. Coat hands in flour and gently press the dough into a rectangle. Fold in half, then press into a rectangle again. Fold in half again, and press into a 12-inch square. Use a knife to cut dough into 16 squares.

3. Place biscuits on a cookie sheet lined with parchment paper. Brush each biscuit with cream. Bake for 18–20 minutes, or until puffed and golden.

Raspberry Cordial

Of course, this isn't real raspberry cordial, or even currant wine, for that matter. We wouldn't want to lose any bosom friends over this, but it is a refreshing drink that will add some sparkle to your Concert on the Green party. SERVES 4-6

In a pitcher or carafe, combine raspberry apple juice concentrate and water. Stir in frozen raspberries and sparkling cider.

½ can raspberry apple juice concentrate

3 cups cold water

1 cup frozen raspberries

1 cup sparkling apple cider

get creative:

Bring an iPod and speakers, and while you wait for the concert to begin, listen to a recording of music similar to what you'll be hearing. Let the children identify each instrument as it plays.

Plum Bars

These cookie bars are my ultimate go-to recipe when I need a casual dessert. I've made them on my blog as Peach Cobbler Bars and Raspberry Jam Bars, but any way I serve them, they're a hit with both kids and adults. The recipe is adapted from my friend Kathy's recipe for Cherry Bars. MAKES 20 BARS

1 stick (8 tablespoons) unsalted butter, at room temperature, plus more for buttering pan

1 cup granulated sugar, plus 3 tablespoons for sprinkling

2 eggs

½ teaspoon pure vanilla extract

½ teaspoon pure almond extract

1½ cups unbleached all-purpose flour

½ teaspoon salt

4 firm but ripe plums

1. Preheat oven to 350°F. Butter a 13 x 9-inch pan or a quarter sheet pan and set aside.

2. In the bowl of an electric mixer fitted with the paddle attachment, cream together butter and 1 cup sugar until smooth and fluffy, about 2–3 minutes. Add eggs, one at a time, incorporating well after each addition. Add vanilla and almond extracts. With the mixer on low, add flour and salt, and mix until just incorporated. Spread the mixture evenly into the prepared pan.

3. Slice plums in half and remove pits. Slice each half into 8 wedges. Arrange plum slices in rows on top of the batter, overlapping each slice as you go along. Sprinkle plums with remaining 3 tablespoons sugar.

4. Bake for 20–25 minutes, or until the edges of the bars are golden brown and the batter is cooked in the center. Allow to cool, and cut into 20 squares.

berry picking party

My parents never took us to Disneyland. They took us to Maine.

I remember bits and pieces of my summers there when I was three and four—a chilly, gray fishing expedition and clam dig with my brother and dad, a trip to the ice-cream shop with my mom and grandmother. I still recall the scent of the perfumed air at our vacation house, and the sunset on the lawn as we played tag with a golden retriever named Sunshine.

One morning, we ventured out to a hill to pick blueberries. I remember sitting amongst the small wild shrubs, as if I came straight off a page from Robert McCloskey's book *Blueberries for Sal*.

Until I was grown, I didn't appreciate how perfect those vacations were—an escape from chores and blistering heat. They were a chance for us to connect with the outdoors, to escape phone calls and television, to read together, and to laugh and talk.

Now, when my own children beg me to take them to Disneyland, I hesitate. Instead, I want them to spend some time in a place where things are slower—a place that has dragged its feet in catching up with the rest of the world.

I want to take them to Maine—back to the place that helped shape who I am. For now, though, I can take them berry picking.

We usually pick raspberries and blackberries, as they do well in our desert summers. But this year, I wanted to do something with blueberries, so we had a Blueberry Picking

RECIPES:
Spicy Sweet Corn Chowder
Sky-High Popovers
Blueberry Refrigerator Jam
Baby Greens Salad with Goat Cheese and Blueberries

books to inspire:

Blueberries for Sal, by Robert McCloskey
Strawberry Girl, by Lois Lenski
JamBerry, by Bruce Degen

Party, even though we had to pick those blueberries at Costco. Sometimes you just have to make do. And that didn't mean we couldn't celebrate.

The first thing we did once we had our cherished bundle of blueberries was to turn on some popular music from the early half of the twentieth century to set the tone. "Blueberry Hill," of course, was on our playlist. We then poured our blueberries into baskets to make them look more beautiful, and measured out the amounts needed to make jam. For lunch, we enjoyed our Spicy Sweet Corn Chowder. When the popovers finished baking, we paired them with some warm jam. They were delicious alongside our salad, which contained whole blueberries and blueberry vinaigrette.

If you're lucky enough to live where blueberries grow wild, find out if the public is allowed to pick them for free. However, since wild blueberries are scarce in most areas of the country, search for local berry farms, which often allow the public to pick their own berries and pay for them by the pound (www.pickyourown.org is a fantastic resource). Ask the kids to print maps and phone numbers and any other necessary information for the day. When you return from the trip, have the children help wash the berries and remove any stems or leaves to begin their involvement with jam making.

music to set the scene:
"Blueberry Hill," by Fats Domino or Louis Armstrong
"Oh Johnny," by the Andrews Sisters
"It's a Good Day," by Perry Como

Spicy Sweet Corn Chowder

Chowder is the perfect make-ahead meal, as its flavor usually improves after a day. Make this chowder the night before berry picking, refrigerate it, and heat it up while you prepare the jam.

My sister used to work for a family that ran a clambake business. Their secret to a good clam chowder was to use lots and lots of onions—even more than you think seems right. Once they're translucent and very tender, they add a sweetness and depth you can't get any other way. SERVES 8-10

1. Slice corn off the cob and set aside. Place the cobs in a pot and cover with 6 cups of water. Bring water to a rolling boil, reduce to a low boil, and cook for 15 minutes. Remove cobs and discard. Strain the corn stock through a sieve lined with a white paper towel or cheesecloth. Reserve stock for later.

2. In a large pot set over low heat, melt butter with olive oil, and add onions. Raise the heat to medium and cook, stirring frequently, until onions are tender and start to caramelize on the edges. Add garlic, cayenne pepper, bell pepper, and flour, and cook for 2 minutes more. Stir in milk, a little at a time, until it resembles a thick sauce.

3. Place potatoes in a medium saucepan and cover with water. Bring to a boil over high heat and cook until tender, about 12 minutes. Drain. Mash about half of the potatoes, and leave the rest intact. Add to the soup pot.

4. Stir reserved corn kernels, corn stock, and chicken broth into the soup. Bring to almost a boil, stirring occasionally. Reduce heat to medium, and allow to simmer until corn is tender, about 10 minutes. Stir in cream. Add salt and pepper to taste.

6 ears of corn, shucked

2 tablespoons butter

2 tablespoons olive oil

3 medium yellow onions, diced

3 cloves garlic, minced

⅛ teaspoon cayenne pepper

1 red bell pepper, diced

3 tablespoons unbleached all-purpose flour

1½ cups milk

5 medium Yukon Gold potatoes, scrubbed and diced

4 cups low-sodium canned chicken broth

½ cup heavy cream

Kosher salt and freshly ground black pepper

Sky-High Popovers

My family never tires of popovers. Buttery, chewy, light, and airy, they are perfect for this meal, whether dipped in the chowder or broken open and slathered with butter and the fresh blueberry jam.

We usually make them in a special popover pan, but if you don't have one, you can bake them in muffin tins. Though they don't puff as high, they're every bit as tasty and wonderful. MAKES 12 POPOVERS

1½ cups unbleached all-purpose flour

1¾ cups milk

1 teaspoon kosher salt

3 large eggs

3 tablespoons melted butter, plus 1½ tablespoons room-temperature butter for buttering the pans

1. In a large bowl, whisk together flour, milk, salt, eggs, and melted butter until smooth. Set aside, and preheat oven to 425°F.

2. While the oven preheats, use the room-temperature butter to generously grease each indentation of the popover pans. When the oven is fully heated, place the buttered pans on the center rack and cover with parchment paper or aluminum foil to keep the butter from spattering. Heat in the oven for 2 minutes.

3. Take the pans from the oven and remove the parchment paper or foil. Pour the batter into the popover pans and fill halfway (or fill three-fourths of each cup if using muffin tins). Place in the oven and bake for 30 minutes. Use the oven light to check progress—do not open the oven door until baking has finished! Serve immediately.

Blueberry Refrigerator Jam

This is something the kids will be delighted to help with—from picking the berries, to adding the sugar, to watching it bubble. Have them be in charge of pulling the plate from the freezer and testing the jam for doneness. Then have them watch in anticipation as you pour the hot jam into jars.

Getting jam to jell can be a funny business, and a challenge for even the most seasoned cooks. If for some reason, your jam doesn't thicken—even after several tests—remove it from the heat and tell everyone it's Blueberry Sauce. It will be every bit as delicious as the jam. MAKES 2 10-OUNCE JARS

1. Place a small ceramic plate in the freezer. Place 2 cups of blueberries in a high-sided saucepan, and mash with a potato masher. Add the remaining blueberries along with the rest of the ingredients. Set the saucepan over medium-high heat, and bring mixture to a boil.

2. Once the blueberries start boiling vigorously enough that the bubbles don't dissipate when you stir, set the timer for 12 minutes and continue boiling the berries at the same rate, stirring frequently.

3. When the jam starts to thicken, pull the plate from the freezer and place a small amount of the jam on the plate. Run your finger through the jam, and if it jells and seems thick, remove the pan from heat. If the jam is not thick enough, place the plate back in the freezer, and continue to cook the jam for a minute or two longer. Test again. Repeat until the jam is thickened.

4. Divide the jam into clean glass jars. Allow to cool for about 2 hours, and top with lids. When the jam cools to room temperature, store in the refrigerator and enjoy within 2 weeks.

5 cups fresh blueberries

Zest of 1 lemon

5 tablespoons freshly squeezed lemon juice

1½ cups sugar

get creative:

Create decorative labels for the blueberry jam that include fun names, the date on which the berries were picked, and the best way to enjoy the contents.

Baby Greens Salad with Goat Cheese and Blueberries

This salad is a cool and refreshing side to the warm, hearty chowder. SERVES 4-6

8 cups baby greens, washed
    and dried

4 ounces goat cheese,
    crumbled

1 cup fresh blueberries

Candied Walnuts (recipe
    follows)

Blueberry Vinaigrette (recipe
    follows)

Arrange the greens, goat cheese, blueberries, and Candied Walnuts on individual plates. Drizzle with vinaigrette.

Candied Walnuts

You can adapt this recipe to turn any kind of nut into candy. MAKES ⅓ CUP

3 tablespoons granulated sugar

¼ cup raw walnuts

1. Line a baking sheet with parchment paper. Sprinkle sugar evenly into a medium nonstick skillet, and place over medium heat. Watch the sugar carefully until it starts to turn into liquid. Swirl the pan carefully to distribute the heat evenly.

2. When the sugar is mostly liquid and starts to turn amber in color, add the walnuts to the pan. Immediately stir the walnuts with a wooden spoon and coat them in the caramelized sugar. Remove from heat.

3. Pour candied walnuts onto the prepared baking sheet, and allow to cool completely. Use a sharp knife to break into smaller pieces.

Blueberry Vinaigrette

½ cup fresh or frozen (and thawed) blueberries

3 tablespoons cider vinegar

¼ cup light olive oil

½ teaspoon kosher salt

1 tablespoon pure maple syrup

Place all the ingredients in a blender, and pulse until well blended.

variations on a theme:
Take the kids to a local farmers' market and have them choose fruits or vegetables to create a favorite dish.

fall

carnival at home

I nearly worshipped my older sister. Eight years my senior, she was the epitome of sophistication and mystery. Of course, telling her this now just makes her laugh, but it was true in my eyes. She was talented and pretty, witty and funny. I wanted desperately to be as cool as she was and to win her attention and favor. Any time she spent with my brother and me felt like heaven.

RECIPES:

Homemade Corn Dogs
Funnel Cakes
Popcorn Balls
Homemade Cream Soda

Once, she decided to plan a family carnival. She set games and attractions around the basement, including a kissing booth, a tossing game, and my absolute favorite: Trip to the Moon. She got the idea from an episode of *Mister Rogers.* To take a trip to the moon, we would lie on our backs on a couch with our feet up to make us feel like astronauts. She strung a cutout picture she had drawn of the moon over the railing at the top of the stairs. Once she yelled "Blast off!" she slowly lowered the moon toward us and wiggled the couch so we felt like we were getting closer. She'd raise the moon back to the top of the railing for our trip back to Earth. I thought she was brilliant.

I decided to host a similar event in our yard. One of our favorite books is *Charlotte's Web,* so for our carnival we were inspired by the county fair where Wilbur wins his special prize. We came up with a few simple attractions: a penny toss, rides on the swing, and, of course, Trip to the Moon. The kids were in charge of the games and handing out prizes, while

get creative:

Trip to the Moon: Ask a child to draw a picture of the moon, cut it out, and punch a hole on the edge. Thread a long string through the hole and drape the moon from a hook or a high tree branch. Have the kids raise and lower the moon over the "astronauts" to create the illusion they are taking a trip to outer space.

books to inspire:

Charlotte's Web, by E. B. White
Olivia Saves the Circus, by Ian Falconer
Ballet of the Elephants, by Leda Schubert, illustrated by
Robert Andrew Parker

I was in charge of making the corn dogs and funnel cakes. Traditional calliope music and Nat King Cole's "Straighten Up and Fly Right" played on the stereo, and passing neighbor kids became curious and joined the fun.

To host a mini carnival, try to keep it simple. It's easy to get overwhelmed, and you may just find that once you leave the kitchen to serve the food, all the events are over and the prizes have all been given away. In order to maximize your time taking part in the carnival itself, cooking and serving the food first is ideal. The popcorn balls and sodas can be made ahead of time, and you can cook the corn dogs and funnel cakes just before the carnival begins. Have the kids wait to start the games until you're ready. If they are old enough to be around hot oil with supervision, have them help in the kitchen.

Homemade Corn Dogs

Though I'm not a fan of store-bought corn dogs, this homemade version is quite good when I use the best ingredients. Since hot oil is very dangerous, I recommend kicking the small children out of the kitchen for this one. MAKES 8 CORN DOGS

1¼ cups flour

½ cup cornmeal

¼ cup brown sugar

1 teaspoon salt

1½ teaspoons baking powder

2 eggs, lightly beaten

⅔ cup milk, or as much as needed to make a smooth, thick batter

8 very good-quality hot dogs

8 cups vegetable oil, for frying

1. In a medium high-sided bowl, whisk together flour, cornmeal, brown sugar, salt, and baking powder. Whisk eggs and half of the milk into the flour mixture. Slowly whisk in remaining milk a little at a time until it makes a smooth, thick batter.

2. Dry off hot dogs with a paper towel, and insert each with a skewer or a thin wooden dowel that measures about 4 inches shorter than the diameter of the pot.

3. Pour oil into a heavy-bottomed stockpot, and set over medium-high heat. When the oil reaches 350°F, coat a hot dog in the batter and slowly lower into the hot oil. The corn dog should turn itself over in the oil, but use a good pair of tongs to help it along as necessary to ensure even cooking. Cook until dough is golden brown and cooked through, about 3–4 minutes. Repeat with remaining hot dogs. Serve with mustard.

music to set the scene:

"Straighten Up and Fly Right," by Nat King Cole
The Circus is Coming: Circus Music for Calliope, Klavier, 1990
"Sugar," by Billie Holiday

Funnel Cakes

At the fair in my hometown, this treat was called "fried dough" and was basically a big flat fried piece of dough drenched in butter and cinnamon and sugar. Funnel cakes are much prettier. MAKES 10 FUNNEL CAKES

1. In a medium bowl, combine flour, sugar, salt, and baking powder. In a separate bowl, whisk together milk, egg, vanilla, and lemon zest. Pour the wet ingredients into the dry ingredients, and whisk until all lumps are gone. Batter should be thick enough that when you scoop it up and let it fall back in the bowl, it sits on the surface of the mixture for a moment before "melting" back together. If the mixture seems too thin, whisk in more flour 1 tablespoon at a time.

2. Fill a large heavy-bottomed stockpot with oil. Set over medium-high heat until oil reaches 360°F.

3. Place batter in a large plastic ziplock bag, and make a small cut in the corner. Squeeze batter into the oil in a circular motion to create a funnel cake about 6 inches in diameter. (If the batter breaks apart into small pieces in the oil, whisk 1–2 tablespoons of flour into the remaining batter, and try again.) Cook for 1 minute on the first side, flip, and cook for 30 seconds more. Remove from the oil with a slotted spoon, and place on a paper towel to drain. Dust with powdered sugar.

1¼ cups flour

2 tablespoons sugar

¼ teaspoon salt

½ teaspoon baking powder

¾ cup milk

1 egg

¼ teaspoon pure vanilla extract

Zest of ½ lemon (about 1 teaspoon)

8 cups vegetable oil, for frying

2 tablespoons powdered sugar, for dusting

Popcorn Balls

I'm not quite sure why I'd never made popcorn balls before our carnival, but they're such a fun and inexpensive treat, I know I'll be making them again and again. MAKES 8–10 POPCORN BALLS

½ cup popcorn, popped, or 2 bags microwave popcorn, popped

1½ cups brown sugar

6 tablespoons butter

½ teaspoon salt

⅓ cup light corn syrup

1 cup sweetened condensed milk

1 teaspoon pure vanilla extract

1. Sift popcorn by tossing it from one bowl to another with your hands. Discard any un-popped kernels that accumulate in the bottom of the bowls. Place sifted popcorn in a very large bowl.

2. In a medium saucepan set over medium-high heat, stir together brown sugar, butter, salt, and corn syrup. Keep stirring until it comes to a mild boil. Add condensed milk and bring back to a boil, stirring constantly. Once mixture starts to boil again, stir constantly for 5–7 minutes, or until it starts to turn slightly darker in color and registers 220°F on a candy thermometer. Remove from heat and stir in vanilla.

3. Pour caramel over the popcorn, and mix with a silicone spatula or wooden spoon until all the popcorn is coated. Allow to cool slightly. With buttered hands, shape into baseball-size balls. Insert a stick into each of the balls (if desired) and press the popcorn firmly around the stick to make it adhere. Allow to rest on a sheet of plastic wrap until completely cool.

variations on a theme:

Throw a neighborhood circus. Invite neighbor kids to show off their own tricks and talents, whether it's a cartwheel or their ability to whistle. If they have pets that can do tricks, invite them to share those, too. All the neighborhood parents can cheer heartily.

Homemade Cream Soda

This soda gets some of its color and flavor from caramelized sugar. It takes a bit of candy-making skill, but is very worth it. You won't need a candy thermometer because the recipe only calls for a little sugar; just keep a keen eye to watch for the sugar to change color. As with any candy making, strict parental supervision is recommended. Since caramelizing sugar is all about timing and precision, please read all instructions before beginning. SERVES 8

1. In a heavy-bottomed saucepan, combine sugar, cool water, and salt. Set over medium-high heat and stir until sugar starts to dissolve. When the mixture starts to boil, stop stirring. From this point on, any stirring should be done by carefully lifting the saucepan and swirling it around.

2. Have the hot water waiting by the stove. Let the syrup bubble away until the sound of popping bubbles changes and the syrup starts to thicken. Swirl the pan as needed to distribute the heat evenly. When the sugar turns a bronzy amber color, remove from heat and stir in hot water and vanilla with a sturdy whisk. The mixture will bubble violently at first, so be very careful. Set over low heat, and whisk until the water and sugar syrup form a cohesive, amber-colored syrup. Allow to cool completely.

3. Place 2 tablespoons syrup in the bottom of a soda bottle or glass, and top with ¾ cup sparkling water and ice, as desired.

1 cup sugar

¼ cup cool water

Pinch of salt

⅓ cup very hot water

1 teaspoon pure vanilla extract

1½ liters sparkling water

back to school breakfast

New shoes always announced the start of a new school year. My mother would buy us new sneakers the week before Labor Day, and the agonizing wait to wear them would begin. My older brother and I would lace them up and place them beside our new, carefully planned first-day-of-school outfits. Sometimes our mom would let us try them on and walk around the house for a few minutes, but we always had to take them off again so as not to scuff them or get them dirty. We would stroke them, imagine how we'd look wearing them. Then my brother and I would compare the "treads" on the soles—whose were cleaner, whose were more interesting, and, most importantly, whose were more likely to make us run faster. Getting ready to go back to school might as well have been getting ready for Christmas.

I want my own children to look forward to the start of school as much as I did. If they can love learning, regardless of their ages and where they are, then I believe they will succeed. I think the best way to foster their love for learning is to celebrate and show my appreciation for it.

A fellow blogger, Stephanie Nielsen, hosts a back-to-school dinner each year for her kids. She inspired me to do something similar. Our Back to School Breakfast—or as I like to call it, our Education Celebration—began the night before. My children set out their clothes and packed their lunches, while I prepared the French toast, raspberry syrup, and Fruit and Nut Muesli Bars. As soon as I woke up the next morning, I placed the French toast and bacon in the oven. Breakfast was ready by the time the kids were out of the shower and ready for the day.

Celebrating the first day of school in your house might work best as a breakfast like ours, but you could also celebrate the evening before. Use the time at the table to help ease any first-day-of-school anxieties and to share personal stories from your own school days.

RECIPES:
Fresh Peach French Toast Bread Pudding
Maple Bacon
Fruit and Nut Muesli Bars

variations on a theme:

To avoid morning chaos, host a special breakfast-for-dinner the night before.

Fresh Peach French Toast Bread Pudding

The inspiration for this bread pudding comes from the Yardley Inn, a bed-and-breakfast in Manti, Utah.
SERVES 6

6 medium peaches, sliced and peeled

¼ cup pure maple syrup, plus 2 tablespoons

3 tablespoons butter, melted

½ teaspoon ground cinnamon

1 tablespoon freshly squeezed lemon juice

1 cup milk

½ cup heavy cream

4 eggs, well beaten

¼ teaspoon nutmeg

1 teaspoon pure vanilla extract

½ teaspoon pure almond extract

6 thick slices artisan bread

1 teaspoon powdered sugar

Raspberry Syrup (recipe follows)

1. Preheat oven to 350°F. Spread peaches out in a single layer in a medium casserole dish or a large pie plate. Combine ¼ cup maple syrup, melted butter, cinnamon, and lemon juice in a small bowl and pour over peaches.

2. In a large bowl, whisk together 2 tablespoons maple syrup, milk, heavy cream, eggs, nutmeg, and extracts. Place bread slices in the mixture and press down so they soak up mixture.

3. Arrange soaked bread on top of the peaches. Pour as much remaining mixture over the bread as will fit in the dish without overflowing.

4. Place the dish on a baking sheet to catch any drips, cover loosely with aluminum foil, and bake for 30 minutes. Remove foil, and bake for 20–25 minutes more, or until a toothpick inserted in the center comes out clean. Dust with powdered sugar, and serve with Raspberry Syrup.

Raspberry Syrup

12 ounces frozen raspberries, defrosted

¼ cup pure maple syrup

Mix the ingredients together and serve, or place in a blender and strain through a fine-mesh sieve.

Maple Bacon

I was never much of a fan of bacon until I discovered this method of baking it. It's sweet and crunchy and salty all at once. What's not to love? SERVES 6

1. Preheat oven to 400°F. Place a piece of parchment paper in the bottom of a rimmed baking sheet, and set a cooling rack on top.

2. Lay the strips of bacon on the cooling rack. Brush each strip with maple syrup. Bake for 18–20 minutes or until crisped to your liking.

1 (12-ounce) package thickly sliced all-natural bacon

¼ cup pure maple syrup

get creative:

Set goals for the coming school year. Give each child a piece of paper and a pen or some crayons, and have them write down what they hope to accomplish in the months ahead. Seal each child's goals in an envelope to be opened and enjoyed on the last day of school.

Fruit and Nut Muesli Bars

Make these treats the night before, and slip them into the kids' lunchboxes along with a love note. One of the beauties of food blogging, is the opportunity to share our ideas with the world, and learn from other talented people as well. I learned this trick—creating a syrup out of sugar, butter, and honey to make chewy granola bars—from Lauren Brennan, of laurenslatest.com, who got the idea from Rachael Ray.
MAKES 16 BARS

1½ cups quick oats

1 cup crisp rice cereal

1 cup mixed nuts

1 cup dried cranberries

1 cup golden raisins

1 cup evaporated cane syrup or brown sugar

1 stick (8 tablespoons) unsalted butter

⅓ cup honey

Pinch of kosher salt

1 teaspoon pure vanilla extract

1. In a large bowl, combine oats, crisp rice cereal, nuts, and dried fruit.

2. In a medium saucepan set over medium heat, combine evaporated cane syrup, butter, honey, and salt. Stir constantly until the mixture reaches 220°F on a candy thermometer. Remove from heat and stir in vanilla. Pour over the oats mixture, and stir to coat well.

3. Press mixture firmly into an 8 x 8-inch square pan, and let sit for 2 hours or overnight. Slice into bars and wrap each in parchment paper. Place one in each lunchbox, and store the rest in an airtight container.

music to set the scene:
Overture to *The School for Scandal*, by Samuel Barber
Rodeo—Four Dance Episodes, by Aaron Copland
"Oh, How I Hate to Get Up in the Morning," by Irving Berlin

books to inspire:
On the Banks of Plum Creek, by Laura Ingalls Wilder
Splat the Cat, by Rob Scotton
Yellowbelly and Plum Go to School, by Nathan Hale

living room sleepover

One Christmas, my little brother received a fantastic toy tepee. Constructed of wooden dowels that nearly reached the ceiling and a rainbow of parachute fabric, it was our own private Xanadu. We set it up in the basement, piled it full of pillows and sleeping bags, and had a sleepover. Our party started with the traditional talking and giggling, but stopped when my little brother zonked out after the first five minutes. My older brother and I soon followed suit. In the middle of the night I awoke, expecting to see colorful panels of fabric above me, but instead found myself draped over my parents' bed. I had sleepwalked all the way there.

Even though my own childhood attempt at a living room sleepover was a bit of a flop, I still love the idea and wanted my kids to experience one. I chose a night when the kids had nothing to do the next morning and I had nothing to do after they fell asleep. Once I said the word, my kids had every last blanket, cushion, and pillow in our home spread out in the middle of the living room in less than eighty-five seconds. I claimed the couch, and let them stake their claims on the floor.

While they set up camp and I cooked the polenta and the mushroom ragout, we listened to "Clair de Lune" by Debussy. I had made the lavender cookies earlier in the day, so they would be ready when we finished our meal and were sipping our Vanilla Spice Steamers.

Our party was simple and quiet, and we took turns reading books to each other until each person drifted off to sleep. I believe I may have been the first to go.

A Living Room Sleepover is such an instinctive way for kids to have fun. It's out of the ordinary routine, yet still in a safe, familiar environment. To celebrate this event with your children, allow them to choose where each person sleeps. Let it be a time to stay up late, whispering and laughing.

RECIPES:
Slow Cooker Creamy Polenta
Mushroom Ragout
Vanilla Spice Steamers
Lavender Star Cookies

music to set the scene:
"Claire de Lune," by Claude Debussy
"The Seal Lullaby," by Eric Whitacre
"Goodnight Moon," by Eric Whitacre

Slow Cooker Creamy Polenta

Creamy polenta is something I learned about as an adult. Made from coarsely ground yellow cornmeal, it's a smooth, comforting starch to serve in place of pasta. Most recipes for polenta are made on the stovetop, but I love using a slow cooker. It's completely hands-off, and works beautifully. If you have leftovers, polenta is wonderful cut into shapes, fried in butter, and sprinkled with sea salt. SERVES 10

8 cups water

2 cups polenta or medium-
   ground yellow corn grits

2 teaspoons kosher salt

1 cup shredded Pecorino
   Romano cheese

3 tablespoons butter

1. Place water, polenta, and salt in a slow cooker and stir. Cover and set the cooker to low. Cook for 6 hours, stirring once after 3 hours, if possible. Turn off slow cooker.

2. Add cheese and butter, and stir until butter is melted. Spoon into bowls, and top with Mushroom Ragout.

Mushroom Ragout

This is one of those recipes I made for myself knowing my kids would probably turn it down. You just have to do that sometimes, you know? If you want to avoid a chorus of "I hate mushrooms," you can serve the polenta with a spoonful of your favorite Bolognese sauce instead. SERVES 4

1. In a large skillet, heat olive oil over medium-low heat. Add the shallot and cook until tender, about 5 minutes. Stir in garlic and cook for 1 minute more. Working in small batches, brown the mushrooms and push them to the outer edge of the pan to make room for the next batch.

2. When all the mushrooms have browned, season with a pinch of salt and pepper and the fresh herbs. Increase heat to medium-high. Pour in sparkling cider, vinegar, and chicken stock. Simmer until liquid is reduced and thickened, about 2 minutes.

3. Spoon on top of polenta, and sprinkle with more fresh herbs and Romano cheese.

2 tablespoons olive oil

1 large shallot, finely minced

1 large clove garlic, finely minced

1 pound mixed mushrooms, such as button, cremini, shiitake, or oyster, thinly sliced

Kosher salt and pepper, to taste

2 teaspoons finely chopped fresh rosemary or thyme, plus more for garnish

¼ cup sparkling cider or white grape juice

½ teaspoon white wine vinegar

½ cup chicken stock

Pecorino Romano cheese, for sprinkling

get creative:

Pull out the flashlight and take turns making shadow puppets. Then, if you're brave, pass it around so each person can tell a ghost story.

Vanilla Spice Steamers

These steamers are just a small, quick shot of something warm and sweet before bed. If you are serving a crowd or want more than a little bedtime snack, double or triple the recipe. MAKES 4-6 ESPRESSO-SIZE SERVINGS

2 cups milk

1 teaspoon cinnamon

½ teaspoon nutmeg

2 tablespoons honey

2 tablespoons sugar

½ teaspoon pure vanilla extract

1. Combine all the ingredients except the vanilla in a medium saucepan set over medium heat. Bring the mixture almost to a boil.

2. Just when little bubbles start to form around the edges of the pan, remove from heat and stir in vanilla. Whisk the steamed milk vigorously to create lots of bubbles, and serve.

books to inspire:

Goodnight Moon, by Margaret Wise Brown
Mother Goose rhymes
The Napping House, by Audrey Wood and Don Wood
Nora's Stars, by Satomi Ichikawa

Lavender Star Cookies

I added lavender to these cookies to give them a sleepy, dreamy kind of taste. The flavor is subtle, merely a hint. I found dried lavender buds at my local health food store and ground them in a coffee grinder.

MAKES ABOUT 2 DOZEN SMALL COOKIES

1¾ cups all-purpose flour

½ teaspoon baking powder

½ teaspoon salt

1 stick (8 tablespoons) unsalted butter, at room temperature

¾ cup granulated sugar

1 egg

½ teaspoon pure vanilla extract

½ teaspoon ground lavender

Royal Icing (recipe follows)

1. In a small bowl, combine flour, baking powder, and salt.

2. In the bowl of an electric mixer fitted with the paddle attachment, cream the butter and sugar for 2–3 minutes, or until pale and fluffy. Add the egg and incorporate until smooth, scraping down the bowl as necessary. Add vanilla and lavender, and mix until well combined. With the mixer on low, add the flour mixture. Stir until just combined.

3. Place dough on a large piece of plastic wrap, and form it into a ball. Place another sheet of plastic wrap on top, and use a rolling pin to roll dough out ¼ inch thick. Use the plastic to slide dough onto a cookie sheet, and refrigerate for 30 minutes, or until firm and cold.

4. Preheat oven to 325°F. Remove plastic wrap and place dough on a lightly floured board. Use cookie cutters to cut dough into shapes, and place them on the cookie sheet about 1 inch apart. Bake for 8–10 minutes, or until almost starting to brown along the edges. Let cool in the pan for a minute or two before transferring to a cooling rack to cool completely. Decorate with Royal Icing.

variations on a theme:

If the weather is warm enough, set up a tent and have a backyard campout. Or keep it inside and use a few chairs or other accessible furniture for draping blankets over to create a cozy sleep fort.

Royal Icing

This is that ultra-white, ultra-versatile frosting. Add a few drops of water at the end of mixing, and you have what you need to create those perfectly smooth frosted cookies. Add enough powdered sugar, and you have glue to hold together a gingerbread house. MAKES ENOUGH TO FROST 24 SMALL COOKIES

1. Place all the ingredients in the bowl of an electric mixer fitted with the whisk attachment. Mix on low speed until the ingredients are well incorporated, raise the speed to medium-high, and beat for 6–7 minutes, or until thick and shiny.

2. For piping and decorating, icing should be stiff and hold its shape. If it is not thick enough, add more confectioner's sugar, 1 tablespoon at a time, and beat with the mixer after each addition until desired consistency is achieved.

3. For flood icing (filling in a whole space with a smooth surface of icing), the icing should fall in ribbons when lifted from the bowl with a spoon, hold its shape for a second or two on the surface, and then "melt" back into itself. Add warm water, 1 teaspoon at a time, and stir with a spoon after each addition until this consistency is achieved.

4. Tint with food coloring as desired. Pour into a piping bag or squeeze bottle, available at craft stores in the cake-decorating aisle. Squeeze frosting around the outer edge of the shape you want to flood with icing, and then fill the shape in with more icing. Use an offset spatula to help smooth out any gaps. Sprinkle with sanding sugar, if desired, while the icing is still wet. Allow icing to dry for 4–6 hours or overnight.

1 pound confectioner's sugar

⅓ cup warm water

2 egg whites, or 4 teaspoons powdered egg whites plus an additional ¼ cup warm water

1 teaspoon pure vanilla extract

pumpkin carving party

One sunny fall day while living in Colorado Springs a few years ago, I had this overwhelming desire to buy a farm in New England and start a pumpkin patch. Within a few minutes of my daydream, I had filled in all the details of the farm, complete with sheep, chickens, Clydesdales, and a golden retriever. The children and I would work to grow the pumpkins, and when they were in school, I would host a knitting circle, where women in the neighborhood would get together to knit sweaters from the wool my sheep would provide.

In my dream we have a small country store with rustic wood floors that make a hollow scuffling sound when you walk on them, and tables to display stacks of jams and an assortment of homemade pies. As people arrive, they can help themselves to mugs of hot apple cider while they wait to take a hayride pulled by the horses.

It is my favorite dream, and I'm still hanging onto it. My youngest child, who desperately loves dogs, has come to know that the day he will get a dog is the day I get my pumpkin patch.

As months speed by, and we discover it is time once again to buy our pumpkins, I feel a twinge of longing for that life I have imagined. Whenever we find a small pumpkin stand run by a local family, we usually buy a few more pumpkins than we need, as a good-faith investment in our future. While we carve our pumpkins, in my heart I am celebrating that future.

For our Pumpkin Carving Party, I got all of the food ready ahead of time so I could be right there when the carving was

RECIPES:

Lemon Sage Drumsticks
Autumn Harvest Salad with
  Pumpkin Seeds
Dunking Cider
Pumpkin Swirl Doughnuts

get creative:

Take children to pick their own pumpkins from a local pumpkin patch. Let them design and carve their own pumpkins with help from adults. Have them sketch their ideas on paper first, then transfer them onto the pumpkins with markers.

happening. I figured it was best not to be in the kitchen when my six-year-old was on the lawn with a host of sharp, pointy objects. Earlier in the day, I had made the dough for doughnuts and toasted the pumpkin seeds for the salad. Right before we went outside, I put the chicken in the oven and set the cider on the stove to warm. That way, when we came inside after finishing our creations, we could scrub slimy pumpkin innards off our hands and arms and get right to dinner.

While we ate, I kept my eye on the pot of oil as it heated for our doughnuts. We indulged as we listened to Brahms's Sonata no. 1 for Violin and Piano, the perfect backdrop to

music to set
the scene:

Brahms's Sonata no. 1 for
Violin and Piano
Danse Macabre, op. 4, by
Camille Saint-Saëns
"The Sorcerer's
Apprentice," by Paul
Dukas
"Funeral March of a
Marionette," by Charles
Gounod

readings of Tasha Tudor's *Pumpkin Moonshine* and Mary Lyn Ray's *Pumpkins: A Story for a Field.*

To throw your own party, carve the pumpkins no earlier than a day before you need the jack-o'-lanterns, so they will be as fresh as possible. If you live where it's warm enough, take advantage and carve your pumpkins outside so that cleanup is easier. (Of course, that suggestion won't work in some parts of the world where the weather seems to think the last week of October is the first week of winter.) If you have a lot of pumpkins to carve, invite some friends to help, including adults!

Lemon Sage Drumsticks

My kids always fight over the drumsticks. Sometimes it's good to just give them what they want. SERVES 6

2 pounds drumsticks

2 tablespoons butter, melted

Olive oil

Kosher salt and freshly ground
    black pepper

5 fresh sage leaves, roughly
    chopped

1 lemon, thinly sliced

Juice from ½ lemon

1. Preheat oven to 450°F. Arrange drumsticks on a wire cooling rack set over a parchment paper–lined baking sheet. Brush chicken with melted butter, drizzle with olive oil, and sprinkle with salt and pepper.

2. Top drumsticks with sage leaves and lemon slices. Squeeze lemon juice over the top of the chicken. Roast for 30–35 minutes, or until chicken skin is golden, the internal temperature is 165°F, and the juices run clear. Allow the meat to rest for 10 minutes, then serve.

variations on a theme:

Host a leaf-raking party! Invite neighborhood kids to bring their own rakes. Serve food after they're done jumping in piles and filling compost buckets with leaves.

Autumn Harvest Salad with Pumpkin Seeds

For this salad, I like to use the pumpkin seeds that are already hulled. They are small and green, and you can find them at the health food store. I also use walnut oil, as it adds an earthier note to the salad, but you can simply use olive oil in its place if it's the only kind you have at home. MAKES 6 SIDE SALADS

1. Preheat oven to 400°F. In a small skillet set over medium-high heat, toast the pumpkin seeds, tossing often and watching carefully to prevent burning. Cook until they start to brown and pop, about 2–3 minutes. Set aside.

2. On a large-rimmed baking sheet, toss cauliflower and parsnips with about 2 tablespoons olive oil and a good pinch of kosher salt and pepper. Bake for 15–20 minutes, or until the cauliflower is browned and the parsnips start to curl.

3. In a large bowl, whisk together vinegar, maple syrup, walnut oil, 3 tablespoons olive oil, and a pinch of salt and pepper. Add the greens, and toss to coat. Top with roasted cauliflower and pumpkin seeds.

¼ cup raw, shelled pumpkin seeds

1 head cauliflower, cut into bite-size pieces

2 parsnips, very thinly sliced

5 tablespoons olive oil

Kosher salt and pepper

3 tablespoons cider vinegar

1 tablespoon pure maple syrup

2 tablespoons walnut oil

2 large handfuls of greens, such as mustard greens, arugula, or a salad mix

Dunking Cider

This spiced cider is simply warmed-up apple cider poured over a spiced herbal tea packet. Nothing could be easier. My personal favorite flavors are Bengal Spice or Cinnamon Apple Spice from Celestial Seasonings. SERVES 6

1. Place a tea bag in the bottom of each of 6 mugs.

2. Heat apple cider until it is almost boiling. Pour over tea bags and let steep for 2 minutes.

6 bags spiced herbal tea

6 cups cold-pressed apple cider

Pumpkin Swirl Doughnuts

Hands down, homemade doughnuts are our family's number one weakness. And how could they not be? Warm and doughy on the inside and crispy and sweet on the outside, they're pure heaven.

Our Pumpkin Carving Party needed the ultimate fall doughnut, so we combined the flavors of cinnamon rolls and pumpkin and came up with these. The dough for these doughnuts is a bit on the sticky side—that's what keeps them soft. Try to add as little flour as possible when you're working with the dough.

MAKES 3 DOZEN BITE-SIZE DOUGHNUTS

4 cups bread flour or unbleached all-purpose flour, plus more for rolling

1 tablespoon instant yeast

½ teaspoon nutmeg

¼ teaspoon ground ginger

¼ cup pure maple syrup

1 egg

¾ cup canned pumpkin

¾ cup warm water (110°F)

2 tablespoons unsalted butter, melted

¾ teaspoon kosher salt

¼ cup powdered sugar

1 tablespoon ground cinnamon

3 tablespoons salted butter, at room temperature

8 cups vegetable oil, for frying

Cream Glaze (recipe follows)

1. In the bowl of an electric mixer fitted with the dough hook, combine flour, yeast, nutmeg, and ginger. In a medium bowl, combine maple syrup, egg, pumpkin, and water, and then pour into dry ingredients.

2. Knead on low speed for 1 minute, then add melted butter and salt. Continue to knead for 10 minutes, or until the dough is smooth and elastic.

3. Place dough on a lightly floured board and knead a few times by hand to form a smooth, cohesive ball. Place in an oiled bowl, cover, and let rise for 40 minutes, or until doubled in bulk.

4. Roll dough out onto a lightly floured board into an 18-inch square. Spread dough with room-temperature butter. Mix sugar with cinnamon and sprinkle over the butter with a fine sieve.

5. Using a sharp knife, cut the dough in half to make 2 rectangles. Roll up each rectangle lengthwise, and pinch along the seam to seal in the cinnamon and sugar. Cut into 1-inch slices to make mini cinnamon rolls. Place on a lightly floured piece of plastic wrap or parchment paper and cover with plastic.

6. Pour oil into a heavy-bottomed stockpot, and set over medium-high heat. When oil reaches 350°F, fry doughnuts—about 4 or 5 at a time—until lightly golden, about 1 minute on each side. Remove from oil with a slotted spoon, and let cool slightly on a paper towel. Dip in glaze, and allow to cool on a cooling rack.

Cream Glaze

Mix together the powdered sugar, cream, and vanilla, and whisk until smooth. Add more liquid as necessary to make a smooth, runny glaze.

2 cups powdered sugar

6–8 tablespoons heavy cream

1 teaspoon pure vanilla extract

rainy afternoon party

When my daughter was two, I splurged and bought her a bright yellow double-breasted slicker with buttons. I couldn't afford the hat that went with it, which was just as well, because the raincoat was impractical anyway. We were living in the Rocky Mountains at the time, and though it did rain every now and then, by the time you got all the raingear on and walked out the door, the sun would be out with puffy clouds smiling innocently down, as if only the sprinklers had wetted the landscape—and that downpour had been just your imagination.

One miraculous day, though, just before the season changed, it rained and drizzled like a perfect New England day. I had Sophie stand out on the balcony of our apartment so she—and mostly I—could enjoy that raincoat, if even for a few minutes. This is all so unlike the days of my own childhood, when the steady clapping of raindrops became a fixture in my ears while it poured for hours and hours. Those days were long, and my brother and I often felt like Sally and her brother from *The Cat in the Hat* as they sat inside on that "cold, cold, wet day." A cat in a striped hat would have been the perfect solution!

Now when it rains like that, I am giddy with childhood memories.

I love that first rainy, cold-to-the-bone day in early autumn that shoos out the mosquitoes and dusty flip-flops of a lingering summer. It marks the start of earlier bedtimes,

RECIPES:

English Pub Onion Soup
Root Vegetable Salad
One-Pan Skillet Brownie
Two-Minute Ganache

music to set the scene:

Piano Concerto no. 5 in F Minor, BWV 1056, by Johann Sebastian Bach
"Somewhere Over the Rainbow," by Harold Arlen and E. Y. Hamburg, and performed by Israel "IZ" Kamakawiwo'ole
"Ain't No Sunshine," by Bill Withers

ruddy cheeks, thick socks, and sweaters. Nothing makes me happier than turning on the heat for the first time in months and curling up with a good book with my kids.

Our Rainy Afternoon Party was therefore very casual. We didn't need to go anywhere or see anybody. It was simply the four of us. I stayed in the kitchen most of the afternoon, making the soup and roasted vegetables, while the kids gathered in the living room to read. They wandered in and out of the kitchen while I cooked, and occasionally I would wander into the living room. We listened to Bach's Piano Concerto no. 5, and its soothing melody helped set a sweet, restful tone for the day. Since my youngest son was not able to read yet, I read snippets from *Winnie the Pooh* to him while the older kids read their chapter books. When my daughter was bored with reading, I had her write up word strips for charades, which we played while we ate dessert.

You can celebrate a rainy day wherever you live. It isn't as much about the weather as it is about reveling in the warmth and comforts of home. Because planning on the weather is next to impossible, this party is meant to be a spontaneous excuse for lazing about and creating memories of leisure and togetherness. Put children in charge of setting the scene. Help them understand the relaxed feeling you are trying to create in the family room, and encourage them to think of ways to accomplish it. Have them gather blankets for curling up in and books to enjoy.

get creative:

Have a board game tournament. Choose a game that is quick and easy for all family members, such as Blink or Spot It, and give out small prizes for participating and winning.

English Pub Onion Soup

My friend's mom loved this soup when she lived in England and begged the pub owner for the recipe. He refused to divulge it until the day she left the country. I have adapted it a little to keep his secret safe. Instead of the dark broth associated with a French onion soup, this recipe produces a broth with a lighter color. MAKES 6 LARGE BOWLS

1. Preheat oven to 400°F. Spread bread cubes out in a single layer on a baking sheet, and toast in the oven for 10 minutes. Remove from oven and set aside.

2. In a large pot set over medium-low heat, melt butter and add onions with a pinch of salt. Cover partially with a lid and let cook, stirring frequently, until onions are very tender, about 15 minutes.

3. Add chicken stock, bouillon paste, and vinegar. Let simmer for 1–2 minutes, and taste for seasoning. Add more kosher salt if needed, and cracked pepper.

4. Ladle soup into ovenproof mugs or bowls set on a baking sheet, and top with the sourdough croutons and a handful of cheese on each serving.

5. Bake until cheese starts to bubble and turn golden brown. Serve hot.

1 loaf rustic sourdough bread, cut into 1-inch cubes

4 tablespoons unsalted butter

3 pounds yellow onions, thinly sliced

Pinch of kosher salt, plus more for seasoning

6 cups homemade chicken stock or good-quality canned chicken broth

1 tablespoon all-natural bouillon paste

1 tablespoon rice wine vinegar

Freshly cracked pepper to taste

2 cups (8 ounces) shredded Gruyère cheese

books to inspire:

Winnie the Pooh, by A. A. Milne
A Wrinkle in Time, by Madeleine L'Engle
Sylvester and the Magic Pebble, by William Steig

Root Vegetable Salad

I love a good toss of warm roasted root vegetables. As they cook, the edges turn to caramel. Leave it to me and my kids to prefer our vegetables to taste more like candy than something healthy. SERVES 6

3 medium golden beets, scrubbed and cut in fourths

1 pound carrots, peeled and cut into 3-inch pieces

1 pound parsnips, peeled and cut into 2- or 3-inch pieces

Olive oil

Kosher salt and pepper

1. Preheat oven to 400°F. Place vegetables on a baking sheet and toss with olive oil, salt, and pepper.

2. Roast for 35–45 minutes, tossing halfway through roasting, until caramelized and tender to the point of a knife.

One-Pan Skillet Brownie

This is a spin-off of a skillet cookie I made for my blog. That cookie, mixed and baked all in one pan, is one of my most popular recipes. I love the idea of dirtying only one pan, so I adapted this recipe into something new. SERVES 4-6

1. Preheat oven to 325°F. Melt butter in an 8-inch cast-iron skillet set over low heat. When butter is completely melted, remove from heat and pour in chocolate chips. Stir chocolate chips until mostly melted.

2. Carefully stir in sugar, vanilla, and salt, and mix until smooth. Add eggs, and whisk mixture with a fork until eggs are completely incorporated. Fold in flour, and stir until combined.

3. Place the skillet in the oven and bake for 30–45 minutes, or until the center is almost set. To serve, scoop out with a large spoon, top with vanilla ice cream, and drizzle with Two-Minute Ganache.

6 tablespoons unsalted butter

1½ cups good-quality semi-sweet chocolate chips

¾ cup sugar

½ teaspoon pure vanilla extract

½ teaspoon kosher salt

2 eggs

½ cup unbleached all-purpose flour

variations on a theme:

If it never seems to rain, celebrate the first blustery day or have a party to celebrate the first day of autumn.

Two-Minute Ganache

Don't ever bother to buy a jar of hot fudge. This ganache is so easy to make that my kids make it for me when they want to surprise me with a treat. MAKES 1 CUP

⅓ cup heavy cream

1 cup very high-quality semisweet or bittersweet chocolate chips

½ teaspoon pure vanilla extract

1. In a small microwave-safe bowl, microwave cream on high for 30 seconds, or until boiling.

2. Add chocolate chips and vanilla. Wait for 1 minute while the chocolate melts, then whisk until smooth and glossy. Refrigerate any leftovers.

winter

fireside supper

In the early days of my marriage, I wistfully mourned not having a house with a real fireplace. I had these romantic notions of a fire burning while reading books and writing letters to distant friends. My daughter would sing arias by the mantelpiece, and my sons would accompany her on the piano and cello. We would be as lovely as a Jane Austen novel. How perfect life would have been if only we had had a fireplace!

Then, recently, we had the good fortune of living in a house with one of the most beautiful fireplaces I have ever seen. Designed and built by my friend, it's surrounded in black slate and polished cherry wood. I thought when we moved in, our fantasy of fireplace-heaven could finally begin. What I soon discovered, though, was that a real fireplace means a lot of real work: starting the fire, which takes a lot longer than one would think when the wood is cold; keeping the fire going—again, not easy when the wood is cold; and cleanup, which nearly broke my vacuum cleaner.

Still, it was nice to have real fires while we lived there. We came to understand that they were best enjoyed on special occasions such as Christmas Day or for our little family dinner party.

What I love about having a dinner party with the kids is that they appreciate all the attention to detail as much as adults do, if not more. They love the candlesticks and center-pieces, the place cards and votives. When we make a dinner party a special occasion, they enjoy dressing up and using their best manners. For our fireside supper, I made special invitations for each of the children a week ahead of time and left them on their beds. This put them in the proper frame of mind to look forward to the event and know that I would expect their best behavior.

Since we have no cook and no butler, we worked together to prepare for the meal. First, we made pasta dough, kneaded it, cut it, and let it rest while everyone helped slide the table into the living room beside the fireplace. As the sauce simmered

RECIPES:
Homemade Fettuccini
Meatballs
Crusty Garlic Bread
Cardamom Rice Pudding

books to
inspire:

The Wind in the Willows,
by Kenneth Graham
Emma, by Jane Austen
The Little White Horse,
by Elizabeth Goudge

with the meatballs, my daughter made the place cards and my sons helped with setting the table and lighting candles. While the water for the pasta came to a boil and the bread warmed up, I lit the fire. Once it was sufficiently roaring, the water was boiling and I started cooking the pasta. Within a few minutes, everything was on the table, and we enjoyed our dinner while listening to a collection of Chopin's Nocturnes.

Nothing tastes quite as glorious as homemade pasta, so we made it for our fancy dinner, but it's not necessary to go to all the trouble. Pasta from a box works just as well. If you don't have a fireplace, try doing something slightly different to make the meal special, such as moving the table to the living room or lighting candles.

Homemade Fettuccini

Homemade pasta is so delicious—it can be enjoyed with a sauce or just a pat of butter and a sprinkling of Parmesan cheese. It can also be a little tricky if you're just starting. But don't panic. It takes a little bit of practice and patience. You may think it's not coming together as it should, but a few passes through the machine, and it will usually work itself out. Just hang in there. SERVES 8

1. In a food processor* fitted with the dough blade, pulse together semolina, all-purpose flour, eggs, olive oil, and a pinch of salt. Hold the food processor with a firm hand, and turn on the machine for 20–30 seconds to knead the dough. Wrap dough in plastic wrap and refrigerate for 30 minutes to rest.

2. Divide dough in fourths. Working with each piece separately, flatten the dough and pass through a pasta roller set to the widest setting. (If the first pass results in a separated mess, don't worry. Simply press all the little scraps into a flat rectangle with your hands, and pass through the roller again. This should make it hold together.) Fold in half, and roll through again. Repeat 3 times. Without folding, pass through again in a single layer, and repeat 3 times. Place the flat sheet of dough on a baking sheet dusted with semolina, and dust the top with more semolina. Cover with plastic wrap. Repeat the same process with the other 3 portions of dough.

3. Set the roller to the next setting. Unwrap and pass each piece through in a single layer 3 times, and place on the semolina-dusted baking sheet to rest. Set the roller to the next setting, and repeat the same process again and again until the dough reaches the desired thickness. If at any time the sheets of dough get too long, cut them in half with a sharp knife.

4. To make fettuccini, roll the dough until it is thin enough to see your hand through it. Spread the dough on a semolina-dusted

1 cup semolina, plus more for dusting

1 cup all-purpose flour

3 eggs

1 tablespoon olive oil

Pinch of kosher salt, plus more for cooking water

1-2 tablespoons salted butter, for tossing

*Alternately, place flour on a board and make a well in the center. Add eggs, oil, and salt. Beat the eggs and slowly draw in the flour until everything is incorporated. Knead dough by hand for 10 minutes.

board, and use a knife to cut it into ½-inch-wide strips, or use a fettuccini cutter. Gather the strips in a loose pile.

5. Bring a large pot of water to a boil, and add 1 tablespoon of kosher salt. Working in batches, drop a handful of noodles into the water, stir, and wait for them to float to the surface. When they float for 10 seconds, remove with a slotted spoon and place in a dish. Toss with a small dab of butter to prevent sticking while you prepare the rest of the pasta. Repeat with remaining noodles. Serve with Parmesan or meatballs and marinara sauce.

Meatballs

In my college days, I worked at a walk-down deli in Provo, Utah. It was there that I learned how to make meatballs by throwing in ingredients without measuring and using tricks like baking the meatballs on parchment paper–lined baking sheets. MAKES ABOUT 20 GOLF BALL-SIZE MEATBALLS

1. Preheat oven to 350°F. Line a large baking sheet with parchment paper.

2. Pulse bread in a food processor until it becomes crumbs. Place crumbs in a small bowl and cover with milk. Let sit for 5 minutes.

3. Place all ingredients, including the bread crumbs and milk, in a large bowl. Use forks or clean hands to combine gently.

4. Shape mixture into meatballs, using your hands or a retractable scoop, and place on the prepared baking sheet. Sprinkle each meatball with a small pinch of kosher salt. Bake for 30 minutes, or until browned and cooked through.

2 pieces white sandwich bread

¾ cup milk

1 pound lean ground beef

1 pound ground pork

½ medium yellow onion, grated

2 cloves garlic, finely minced

1 egg, lightly beaten

1 cup freshly grated Parmesan or Pecorino Romano cheese

5 fresh basil leaves, torn

¼ cup chopped fresh parsley leaves

1 tablespoon tomato paste

¼ teaspoon freshly ground pepper

Pinch of kosher salt, plus more for sprinkling

variations on a theme:
If you are without a fireplace, candlelight will make just as dazzling an impression, or you can gather around an outside bonfire.

Crusty Garlic Bread

When I lived in Canada, a woman used to invite my friend and me to dinner quite regularly. It was from her that I learned what a difference fresh herbs and other fresh ingredients make in cooking. This is how she made garlic bread. SERVES 6

½ loaf rustic Italian bread, cut into ½-inch slices

4 tablespoons salted butter, melted

3 cloves garlic, finely minced or pushed through a garlic press

3 basil leaves, torn

2 tablespoons chopped fresh flat-leaf parsley

½ cup grated Parmesan or Pecorino Romano cheese

½ cup grated mozzarella cheese

1. Preheat oven to 400°F. Place slices of bread on a baking sheet.

2. Combine melted butter, garlic, basil, parsley, and Parmesan or Pecorino Romano cheese in a small bowl. Spoon onto bread slices, and top with mozzarella.

3. Toast in oven for 12–15 minutes, or until cheese is melted and the bread is toasted on the edges.

get creative:

Ask children to design place cards for each person at the table, using colored pencils or calligraphy pens, stickers, stamps, or stencils, and set the table with special dishes.

Cardamom Rice Pudding

Cardamom is one of my favorite spices. I love it in savory Indian dishes and some spiced desserts. To make this recipe even easier, place all the ingredients into a slow cooker and cook on low for 4 hours.

SERVES 6–8

1. With a sharp paring knife, slice the vanilla bean down the center and scrape out the seeds with the blade. Place the seeds and the scraped pod in a large high-sided skillet.

2. Add the remaining ingredients to the skillet and set over medium-high heat. Bring to a boil, stirring occasionally and watching carefully that the mixture does not scorch. As soon as the mixture begins to boil, reduce the heat to a mild simmer, and cook until rice is tender and pudding thickens, about 20–25 minutes.

3. Remove the empty vanilla bean pod. Spoon pudding into bowls and serve warm, or refrigerate until chilled.

1 vanilla bean

4 cups milk

½ cup arborio or short-grain rice

½ teaspoon ground cardamom

⅓ cup sugar

Pinch of salt

music to set the scene:

Chopin Nocturnes
Le Nozze di Figaro: "Voi Che Sapete," by Wolfgang Amadeus Mozart (my favorite recording is by Magdalena Kožená)
"Was Mir Behagt, ist Nur die Muntre Jagd," by Johann Sebastian Bach (again, I love the recording by Magdelena Kožená)

candy
factory

I spent 10 percent of my youth in pursuit of candy. A short distance from our house, a small store shared a building with our neighborhood post office. Although the sign read "general store," all the kids knew it as "the candy store," "the beehive," or, most often, and most affectionately, The Little Store.

The genius of The Little Store's business model was certainly its proximity to the post office, and the mutually beneficial trade between parents and their children. On a daily basis, parents would send their children to mail off letters, buy stamps, and check post office boxes, all for whatever spare change was in their pockets. Basically, the neighborhood had a whole personnel of couriers who would work for pennies. And my friends and I gladly took the job. We would take several walks to The Little Store each week, filling brown paper sacks with as much candy as we could—Sour Patch Kids, Swedish Fish, Jolly Ranchers, Boston Baked Beans, and Mary Janes. We'd then stop back in at the post office to pick up the mail, and jam the letters in beside the candy.

So, when my teacher read *Charlie and the Chocolate Factory* to my second grade class, I could relate to Willy Wonka's obsession with candy. That obsession remains. As much as I'd like to abandon my sugar cravings, they're always with me, and apparently I've managed to pass them along to my kids. So I figure, until we manage to break free from our candy dependency, why not just embrace it?

For our little Candy Factory celebration, we read *Charlie and the Chocolate Factory* together and did some experimenting in the kitchen. Candy making is somewhat of an art and requires some patience and practice, so we started with the Whipple Scrumptious Fudgemallow Delight Bars—something the kids could make without much help. Once those were in the refrigerator, I demonstrated for them how to make homemade caramels. While the candy set, we had our

RECIPES:
Cabbage and Kale Minestrone
Rustic Rosemary Olive Oil Bread
Whipple Scrumptious
  Fudgemallow Delight Bars
Sour Cream Caramels

music to set the scene:
Chocolat (Original Motion Picture Soundtrack), by Rachel Portman
Charlie and the Chocolate Factory (Original Motion Picture Soundtrack), by Danny Elfman
"I Want Candy," by Bow Wow Wow

lunch of Cabbage and Kale Minestrone and Rustic Rosemary Olive Oil Bread—a feast fit for Charlie Bucket and his family.

When hosting your own Candy Factory party, you can use these recipes or your own family favorites. Since most of the party will be spent in the kitchen learning a new skill, go over rules of safety together, such as keeping pot handles turned in, away from the reach of small children; keeping long hair tied back; and using potholders.

books to inspire:

Charlie and the Chocolate Factory, by Roald Dahl
The Candymakers, by Wendy Mass
The Candy Shop Wars, by Brandon Mull

Cabbage and Kale Minestrone

The Bucket family, in Charlie and the Chocolate Factory, *live on cabbage soup. I can't think of a better or healthier contrast to the candy than a simple bowl of cabbage soup for our party. I added a few more vegetables to make it heartier.* SERVES 12

3 tablespoons good olive oil

1 large yellow onion, diced

1 shallot, diced

Pinch of kosher salt

Pinch of crushed red pepper flakes

2 cloves garlic, chopped

1 teaspoon dried thyme, or 2
   teaspoons fresh thyme

2 bay leaves

4 cups low-sodium chicken broth
   or vegetable broth

1 (28-ounce) can diced tomatoes

1 (15-ounce) can white beans, such
   as cannellini or great northern,
   rinsed and drained

1 small head Napa cabbage,
   chopped

1 bunch kale, washed, ribs
   removed, and chopped

1 teaspoon balsamic vinegar

½ pound small pasta, such as
   tubettini or elbow macaroni,
   cooked al dente

Grated Pecorino Romano or
   Parmesan cheese, for garnish

1. Heat oil in a large pot set over medium heat. Add onions and shallot, and sprinkle with salt. Raise heat to medium-high and cook, stirring often, until onions are tender and the edges turn very brown. Stir in pepper flakes, garlic, thyme, and bay leaves, and cook 1 minute more, being careful not to burn the garlic.

2. Add broth and tomatoes and bring mixture to a boil, then lower heat to medium and allow to simmer for 20 minutes. Add beans and cabbage and cook for another 10 minutes. Right before serving, stir in kale and vinegar.

3. Place a small amount of the cooked pasta into each bowl, ladle some of the soup on top, and garnish with Parmesan cheese.

Rustic Rosemary Olive Oil Bread

This bread was inspired by Jim Lahey's recipe for No-Knead Bread in the New York Times *that took the foodie world by storm a few years ago and changed the way home cooks make bread. My recipe is different, but I could not have come up with it without his genius.*

To make this, you will need a pot of some kind, with a lid, that can withstand a 450°F oven. This could be a Dutch oven or a cast-iron pot with enamel coating, as long as the handles won't melt at high temperatures. I have a special baking stone with a high lid that works beautifully. MAKES 1 LOAF

1. In a large bowl, stir together flour, yeast, salt, water, olive oil, and rosemary. Cover bowl with plastic wrap and let sit for 18–20 hours.

2. Dump dough onto a well-floured board. Take the same bowl that just held the rising dough and dust generously with more flour (the flour should stick to whatever moisture was left behind from the dough). Use very wet hands or a bench scraper to fold the outer edges of the dough into the center a few times to shape into a soft ball. Shape the dough into a taut lump, and return to the floured bowl. Sprinkle a little more flour around the edges of the dough. Cover with plastic, and let rise for 2 hours.

3. While dough is rising, place the Dutch oven or covered pot in the oven, and preheat to 450°F. When the oven comes to temperature, pull out the Dutch oven, lift the lid, and dust the bottom with semolina. Use a silicone spatula or a wooden spoon to ease the dough onto the semolina. Replace the hot lid, and place in the oven for 30 minutes. Remove the lid, and bake for 10 minutes more.

4. Take the bread out of the pot, and place on a cooling rack for 10 minutes. Slice and serve with butter or olive oil.

3 cups bread flour, plus more for dusting

¼ teaspoon instant yeast

1½ teaspoons kosher salt

1¼ cups lukewarm water

¼ cup very good extra-virgin olive oil

1–2 tablespoons fresh rosemary leaves, chopped or left whole

2 tablespoons semolina or cornmeal for dusting the bottom of the pot

Whipple Scrumptious Fudgemallow Delight Bars

Could Roald Dahl have come up with a more enticing name for a chocolate bar? Anytime my kids and I read Charlie and the Chocolate Factory *and we read about Whipple Scrumptious Fudgemallow Delight Bars, I have a sudden craving for one, but we've never found a store-bought candy that could live up to the name. I think these candy bars may just be the solution. This recipe is easy enough that older children can make it with minimal supervision.* MAKES 3 DOZEN CANDY BARS

1 (12-ounce) bag (2 cups) semi-sweet chocolate chips

1 stick (8 tablespoons) unsalted butter

3 tablespoons corn syrup

Pinch of kosher salt

1 (7-ounce) jar (about 2 cups) marshmallow cream

1. Line an 8 x 8-inch square pan with an 8 x 12-inch piece of parchment paper or wax paper so that the paper overlaps the sides of the pan. Hold in place with bulldog or binder clips.

2. Pour chocolate chips, butter, corn syrup, and salt into a large microwave-safe bowl. Microwave on high for 45 seconds, stir, then microwave again for 30-second intervals, stirring well after each, until the chocolate is smooth and shiny.

3. Spread half of the chocolate mixture in the bottom of the prepared pan. Drop marshmallow cream by spoonfuls onto the chocolate. Pour remaining chocolate on top, and use a butter knife to swirl the marshmallow cream into the chocolate. Refrigerate for 2–3 hours.

4. Use a knife to cut the chocolate away from the edges of the pan, and use the excess parchment paper to carefully lift the candy from the pan. Use a sharp knife to cut into 36 squares.

variations on a theme:

Take the family to see a real candy factory if one is close by, or find an old-fashioned candy store and have a party with your purchases.

Sour Cream Caramels

Making caramel is a great way to really experience candy making. The secret is in the temperatures, but it also requires some timing, patience, and precision. Don't panic if you make a mistake the first couple of times you try it. My first attempt at caramel burned, and I had to throw it out and start over. But eventually I got the hang of it.

This recipe requires stirring the caramel with the thermometer in the saucepan. I would recommend investing in a professional candy thermometer, which costs about $12 and can withstand getting knocked around in the pan a bit. The inexpensive glass models probably aren't up to the task. MAKES 32 CANDIES

1. Line an 8 x 8-inch nonstick cake pan with an 8 x 12-inch piece of parchment paper so the edges come up and overlap the sides of the pan.

2. In a large microwave-safe liquid measuring cup, combine sour cream, heavy cream, and vanilla. Microwave on high for about 60–90 seconds, until hot and almost bubbling. Keep at the ready.

3. In a medium heavy-bottomed saucepan, stir together sugar, corn syrup, water, and salt. Set over medium-high heat, and stir occasionally until the syrup starts to bubble. Use a pastry brush dipped in water to brush any sugar crystals down the sides of the pan. Once the syrup bubbles, stop stirring. If you need to redistribute the heat, lift the pan and gently swirl the syrup around. Clip a candy thermometer to the side of the pan, and wait for the heat to reach 305°F.

4. Remove from heat, and with a long-handled wooden spoon, stir in warm cream mixture and butter. The mixture will bubble violently. Be careful and keep stirring. Return to the burner, and keep heat at medium-high. Stir constantly until caramel reaches 240°F (soft ball stage), about 25 minutes. If you don't have a candy thermometer, you can test the doneness by spooning a small amount of the caramel into a glass of cool water. When the candy sinks to the bottom and forms a ball that has the consistency of Silly Putty, you have reached the right stage.

3 tablespoons sour cream

1¼ cups heavy cream

1 teaspoon pure vanilla extract

1½ cups pure cane sugar

3 tablespoons corn syrup

¼ cup water

½ teaspoon kosher salt or sea salt

3 tablespoons unsalted butter, at room temperature

5. Pour into the prepared pan, but do not scrape out the saucepan, as the caramel stuck to the sides is a slightly higher temperature than what slides out of the saucepan easily. Scraping it out will produce caramels that aren't as smooth as they could be. Place the pan on a cooling rack and do not disturb for 5 hours, then place in the refrigerator for 20 minutes. Use a plastic knife to separate the caramel from the sides of the pan, and lift out the caramel with the overhanging parchment paper. With a sharp knife, cut into 32 caramels (8 by 4). To store, wrap in small rectangles of wax paper, parchment paper, or cellophane.

For a variation of this recipe, which results in a firmer caramel that holds its shape and isn't quite as chewy, follow all the same instructions, but take the caramel off the heat at 250°F instead of 240°F in step 4. Cut into squares instead of rectangles, and sprinkle with a small pinch of fleur de sel.

get creative:
Find interesting and beautiful ways to wrap the candy, using small boxes from the craft store, cellophane, scrapbook paper, and ribbons.

snow day

Snow days make life worth living. They are the spontaneous vacation days, proof of divine intervention for the unprepared student. When I was young, my brother and I would hold our breaths as we listened to a crackling AM radio station for school cancellations. When our town was announced, we'd dance around and shout for a few moments before going outside to play.

We would make snowmen, which always ended up full of leaves if it snowed before we got around to raking. Sometimes we made forts and igloos in the snowbanks at the end of our driveway. After playing outside, I would sit on my bed, with my feet propped on the radiator and in a trance, watching the snowflakes in their silent, steady fall to earth. It was a drifting, dreamy feeling.

RECIPES:
Cowboy Food (aka Classic Chili)
Sipping Chocolate
Ginger Clove Biscotti

Where my children and I live now, snow days apparently are a myth. From what I gather, our school district wouldn't cancel school if it snowed 4 feet in one night and the power went out. But we won't give up hoping for one.

This party celebrates the freedom of a schedule wiped clean: no homework, no driving, no lessons, and no after-school sports—the joys of an open-ended day. It celebrates the kissable red cheeks of a child warming up in the kitchen, or the sun breaking through the clouds over a sparkling white carpet of snowflakes.

This celebration is pure spontaneity. The goal is not structure, by any means, but rather good casual food, lots of smiles, and random singing for joy throughout the day—"It's a snow day!" Though we haven't had an honest-to-goodness-no-school-snow-day since the last place we lived, we were able to celebrate the snow on a weekend. I left a pot of chili and some Sipping Chocolate on the stove all day to keep us warm while the kids came in and out of the house.

You may want to adapt your Snow Day celebration to your own situation. If you have older children, for example, a great breakfast might be just the right incentive for them to roll out of bed. Use the time to connect with them through conversation that you normally don't have time for on a regular school day. Get them to open up about their classes, their crushes, and their teachers and schoolmates.

books to inspire:

Stopping by Woods on a Snowy Evening, by Robert Frost, illustrated by Susan Jeffers
Brave Irene, by William Steig
Sun and Moon, Ice and Snow, by Jessica Day George
The Mitten, by Jan Brett
The Snowy Day, by Ezra Jack Keats

Cowboy Food (aka Classic Chili)

Chili is the perfect food to make on a snow day. Since nearly everything is something you might have on hand in the fridge and cupboards, you might be able to make it without a trip to the store. I named chili "cowboy food" in our house in my attempt to get my four-year-old son to eat it. Surprisingly, it worked.
SERVES 6

1. In a large pot set over medium heat, sauté beef until it begins to brown. Add onion and stir occasionally until beef is cooked through and onions are tender, about 10 minutes. Stir in garlic, peppers, spices, cocoa powder, and salt, and cook for 2–3 minutes more.

2. Raise the heat to medium-high, and add tomatoes, tomato paste, and beans. Bring the chili to a simmer, stirring occasionally. Lower the heat to medium-low, and simmer for 20 minutes, or until ready to serve.

3. Spoon into bowls, and garnish with cheese, avocado, sour cream, and cilantro.

1 pound ground beef

1 medium yellow onion, finely chopped

2 cloves garlic, peeled and chopped

1 yellow bell pepper, chopped

1 green bell pepper, chopped

1 teaspoon chipotle chili pepper

2 teaspoons ground cumin

½ teaspoon ground cinnamon

Pinch of cayenne pepper

½ teaspoon cocoa powder

1 teaspoon kosher salt

1 (28-ounce) can fire-roasted tomatoes

1 (4-ounce) can tomato paste

1 (14-ounce) can dark red kidney beans

Shredded sharp cheddar cheese, for garnish

Chopped avocados, for garnish

Sour cream, for garnish

Chopped fresh cilantro, for garnish

music to set the scene:

"Rêverie," by Claude Debussy
Trois Gymnopédies: "Gymnopédie No. 1" (Lent et Douloureux), by Erik Satie
Concerto no. 20 in D Minor for Piano and Orchestra, by Wolfgang Amadeus Mozart

Sipping Chocolate

This is a thick, rich hot chocolate, and whenever I make it, I imagine I'm drinking what they served on the Polar Express. SERVES 6

4 cups low-fat milk

¼ cup dark or Dutch process cocoa powder

¼ cup sugar

1 teaspoon pure vanilla extract

½ cup semisweet chocolate chips

1. In a medium saucepan, whisk together milk, cocoa powder, and sugar until the cocoa dissolves into the milk. Set over medium heat, and cook until almost boiling.

2. Remove from heat and add vanilla and chocolate chips. Let rest for about 1 minute. Whisk entire mixture briskly and pour into mugs. Top with spoonful of Cinnamon Whipped Cream.

Cinnamon Whipped Cream

½ cup heavy cream

1 tablespoon powdered sugar

½ teaspoon pure vanilla extract

¼ teaspoon ground cinnamon

With an electric mixer, beat all the ingredients together until soft peaks form.

variations on a theme:

Have a winter picnic, whether you have snow or not. Pack hot food, such as mini potpies, and keep warm by heating a clay brick in the oven and wrapping it in a kitchen towel. Bring along a thermos of Sipping Chocolate.

Ginger Clove Biscotti

Biscotti are Italian cookies that are baked twice. They're crunchy and perfect for dipping in hot chocolate. MAKES ABOUT 2 DOZEN COOKIES

1. Preheat oven to 350°F. Line an 11 x 17-inch baking sheet with parchment paper.

2. In a medium bowl, whisk together flour, baking powder, salt, cinnamon, and cloves. Set aside.

3. In the bowl of an electric mixer fitted with the paddle attachment, cream together butter and orange zest. With the mixer on low, slowly pour in sugar, and cream on medium speed until pale, about 2 minutes. Pour in molasses and mix until combined. Add eggs, one at a time, incorporating well after each and scraping down the bowl, if necessary.

4. With the mixer on low, slowly add the dry ingredients. Mix until just combined. Stir in candied ginger.

5. Shape the dough into 2 rectangular logs, measuring about 3 x 15 inches. Place on the parchment-lined baking sheet about 4 inches apart. Bake at 350°F for 20 minutes, until edges are barely turning brown. Allow to cool for 30 minutes.

6. Reduce oven temperature to 300°F. With a serrated knife, cut logs diagonally into 1-inch slices. Place on parchment-lined baking sheet, cut sides up, and bake for 10 minutes. Flip each cookie, and bake for an additional 10 minutes. Cool completely.

7. Line a baking sheet with parchment paper. Place chopped white chocolate in a microwave-safe bowl. Microwave on high for 30-second intervals—stirring well after each—until completely melted.

8. Dip the bottom of each cookie in the white chocolate and place on the parchment-lined baking sheet. Drizzle with more white chocolate and sprinkle with candied ginger. Refrigerate until the chocolate is set, about 30 minutes.

3 cups unbleached all-purpose flour

2½ teaspoons baking powder

½ teaspoon salt

1 teaspoon cinnamon

¾ teaspoon cloves

4 tablespoons butter

2 teaspoons orange zest

1 cup granulated sugar

⅓ cup molasses

2 eggs

½ cup candied ginger, finely chopped, plus more for sprinkling

6 ounces white chocolate, chopped

get creative:

Make a snowman gallery. Depending on how much snow you have, invite each family member to build his or her own snowman or make one together.

care
and
share
breakfast

My kids and I will never forget what happened our first December after the divorce. We weren't necessarily having a sad holiday—I was busy with my blogging work, and the kids were involved with school—but we were still thousands of miles away from all my extended family, and I felt like a one-man band trying to create some sort of Christmas magic all by myself. I was stressed, exhausted, and not feeling much like pulling everything together.

But one night a couple of weeks before Christmas, we heard a knock on our door. Outside was a bag full of small toys and candy—my favorite candy—with a note that said "Day 1." The kids were thrilled, and I was stunned. Each thing inside the bag was special and well thought out. Twelve more nights followed, and every evening the kids would wait and listen for that glorious knock on the door, then run to see what arrived.

On Christmas Eve, we discovered a large and final gift for our Twelve Days of Christmas, along with another sack of gifts from another neighbor. It remains a mystery which of our neighbors gave us the gifts, and it will likely stay that way. We wish we had a way to thank them, but the best we can do is pass it along.

I took inspiration for our Care and Share Breakfast from the 1994 version of *Little Women*. I love that scene when the March girls take their entire Christmas breakfast to the Hummels. On their way, they sing "Here We Come A-Wassailing." We wanted to do something similar to pass along the kindness our secret neighbors had given, so we found a family in our neighborhood that could use some extra cheer and put together a breakfast for them. We made enough Kid-Friendly Wassail, Sausage and Pepper Breakfast Strata, Cranberry Orange Crumb Cake, and Maple Vanilla Crunch Granola for their family and ours. We packed their portion in a large basket, left it on their doorstep, and ran.

RECIPES:
Kid-Friendly Wassail
Sausage and Pepper Breakfast Strata
Cranberry Orange Crumb Cake
Maple Vanilla Crunch Granola

music to set the scene:

Symphony no. 9 in E Minor, op. 95, *From the New World*, "Largo," Part I, by Antonín Dvořák
"Here We Come A'wassailing," Traditional English Carol
The Nutcracker, by Tchaikovsky

get creative:

Have fun deciding how best to package the breakfast foods, such as a cellophane bag with a ribbon for the granola, or a vintage thermos for the wassail. Be sure to include labels for each homemade food item with a list of ingredients that would alert the recipient to any potential allergens.

When we returned home, we enjoyed what we had reserved for ourselves.

There are countless ways to serve within your own community, whether it's helping a neighbor, participating in a local Secret Santa program during the holidays, or volunteering time at a homeless shelter or food bank. Children will learn the deep importance of community service by sharing in these activities together. While you do so, talk about how it makes you feel when you give to others.

Kid-Friendly Wassail

Real, or traditional, wassail dates back to the Middle Ages in England, and was typically brewed from apples and spices. I used citrus juices in my version, which make it lighter and brighter. SERVES 8

Bring all the ingredients to a boil in a large pot. Reduce heat to a simmer, and let cook for about 10 minutes. Serve in mugs.

4 cups white grape juice

2 cups orange juice

Juice of 1 lemon

Juice of 1 lime

1 lime, thinly sliced

1 lemon, thinly sliced

1 orange, thinly sliced

4 cinnamon sticks

4–5 star anise pods

Sausage and Pepper Breakfast Strata

For our Care and Share Breakfast, I needed a breakfast recipe that was highly portable. I remembered a recipe Giada De Laurentiis made on her show Everyday Italian, *where she baked a breakfast strata in a hollowed-out loaf of foccacia bread. It was perfect for our party, so I borrowed her idea.* SERVES 6

1-pound loaf rustic bread, available at good bakeries, or the Rustic Rosemary Olive Oil Bread on page 181

½ pound breakfast sausage

1 small yellow onion, finely chopped

½ orange bell pepper, chopped

½ green bell pepper, chopped

5–7 eggs

2 tablespoons milk

Kosher salt and pepper

½ cup shredded sharp cheddar cheese

1 ounce cream cheese, cut into small pieces

1. Preheat oven to 350°F. Use a sharp knife to carve out the top of the loaf of bread, leaving a ½-inch edge around the top perimeter of the loaf. Pull off the top crust of the bread, and use your fingers to hollow out the center. Save the center of the bread for another use. Place hollowed-out loaf on a parchment paper–lined cookie sheet.

2. In a large skillet set over medium heat, cook the sausage until it starts to brown. Add onions, and continue to cook until the onions start to turn translucent, about 5 minutes. Add peppers, and continue to cook until onions are tender, about 5 minutes more.

3. Beat eggs with milk and a pinch of salt and pepper. Spread sausage mixture into the bottom of the hollowed-out bread and top with cheddar cheese. Pour egg mixture over the top, and dot with cream cheese.

4. Bake for 30–35 minutes, or until a toothpick inserted in the center comes out clean. Allow to cool for 5 minutes, then slice with a serrated knife and serve.

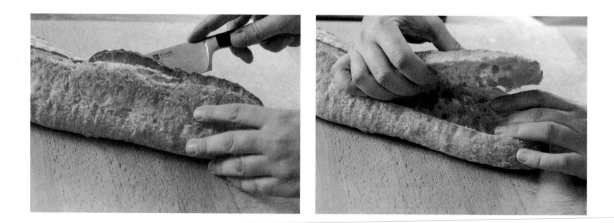

Cranberry Orange Crumb Cake

With all the steps in this recipe, these cakes really are a labor of love. But trust me, they are worth every second. MAKES 2 MEDIUM LOAVES

For the streusel topping:

¾ cup unbleached all-purpose flour

1 cup brown sugar

½ teaspoon salt

¾ teaspoon cinnamon

½ teaspoon ground cardamom

⅛ teaspoon cloves

½ teaspoon nutmeg

6 tablespoons butter

For the cranberry layer:

1 cup fresh or frozen cranberries, roughly chopped

Zest of 1 orange (about 2 tablespoons)

1 tablespoon orange juice

variations on a theme:

Instead of leaving the gifts on a doorstep, invite the family to your home so you can enjoy the meal together.

1. Preheat oven to 350°F. Butter and flour two medium loaf pans.

2. Make the streusel topping by combining flour, sugar, salt, and spices in a medium bowl. Cut butter in small pieces and toss to coat in the sugar and spice mixture. Using a pastry cutter, two knives, or your hands, break up butter into very small pieces until the mixture resembles coarse meal.

3. For the cranberry layer, stir together cranberries, orange zest, and orange juice in a small bowl.

4. To make the cake, whisk together flour, baking powder, baking soda, and salt in a medium bowl. Set aside. In the bowl of an electric mixer fitted with the paddle attachment, cream together butter and sugar and beat until fluffy, about 2 minutes. Add orange zest. With the mixer on medium-low, add eggs, one at a time, incorporating well before adding the next egg. Scrape down the bowl as necessary. Add vanilla.

5. With the mixer on low, add about a third of the dry ingredients. Then add half of the sour cream and the orange juice, followed by the next third of the dry ingredients. Add the remainder of sour cream, and end with the last of the dry ingredients. Mix on low speed until just combined.

6. Divide most of the batter (about two-thirds) evenly between the two loaf pans. Divide the cranberry mixture between the two pans, and top with some of the streusel topping. Layer on the last bit of batter, and top both cakes with the remaining streusel topping. Bake for 30–35 minutes, or until a toothpick or skewer inserted in the center comes out clean.

7. Whisk together all the ingredients for the glaze. Invert the cakes onto a cooling rack, and drizzle with half of the glaze while still warm. Let cool for 20 minutes, and drizzle with the remaining glaze. Serve warm or at room temperature.

For the cake:

2¼ cups unbleached all-purpose flour

1½ teaspoons baking powder

½ teaspoon baking soda

½ teaspoon salt

10 tablespoons unsalted butter

1½ cups sugar

1 tablespoon orange zest

3 eggs

2 teaspoons pure vanilla extract

1 cup sour cream

2 tablespoons freshly squeezed orange juice

For the glaze:

2 tablespoons orange juice

Zest of ½ orange (about 1 tablespoon)

2 tablespoons butter, melted

1 cup powdered sugar

Maple Vanilla Crunch Granola

I love a good crunchy granola, and have been in search of a homemade recipe that has the same crunch that you typically find in the store-bought varieties. I discovered coconut oil is the key. If you would rather not use coconut oil, a vegetable oil will also work, but the granola will be slightly chewier. SERVES 12

6 cups rolled oats

⅓ cup flax seeds or flax meal

½ cup coconut oil, melted,* or 1 cup vegetable oil

1 cup pure maple syrup

½ cup brown rice syrup or honey

2 teaspoons pure vanilla extract

1. Preheat oven to 350°F. Line a rimmed baking sheet with parchment paper or a silicone baking mat. Set aside.

2. Place rolled oats in a large mixing bowl. Grind flax seeds in a coffee grinder until all seeds are broken up, and add to the bowl. Add melted coconut oil or vegetable oil to the bowl, along with maple syrup, brown rice syrup, and vanilla. Stir until everything is well incorporated.

3. Pour granola onto the baking sheet, and bake at 350°F for 10 minutes. Use a spatula to gently flip the granola in the baking sheet to ensure even browning. Reduce heat to 300°F and bake for 10–15 minutes more, or until it starts to turn golden brown.

4. Remove from oven and use a silicone spatula to press the granola firmly into the baking sheet (this will help it form clusters). Let cool completely, then break into pieces. Store in an airtight container for up to 2 weeks, or freeze for up to 2 months.

*To melt coconut oil, place in a microwave-safe liquid measuring cup and microwave on high for 20 seconds. Stir. Microwave in 10-second intervals until fully melted.

books to inspire:

Little Women, by Louisa May Alcott
A Little Princess, by Frances Hodgson Burnett
The Little Match Girl, by Hans Christian Andersen

tree trimming party

My dad hated setting up the Christmas tree. I can still see him, red-faced, holding his breath and grumbling. Because that tree . . . had . . . to . . . be . . . straight. I'm surprised he never had a heart attack.

RECIPES:
Cranberry Glazed Ribs
Light as Air Mashed Potatoes
Parker House Rolls
Pear-y Cherry Crumble

He always did get the Christmas tree to stand perfectly straight, though. One year he sawed off all extraneous branches and relocated them into carefully spaced holes he drilled into the trunk. Another year, after the tree was perfectly positioned and decorated, he wanted to move it onto a platform with a train track that ran around the perimeter. When it was where he wanted it, the tree came crashing down, along with most of the glass ornaments. That was a low point.

The first time I had to put up the tree by myself felt like an out-of-body experience. Every time I shouted to the kids, with my hand on a sappy trunk and my face full of branches, "Is it straight? Is it straight?!" I knew I looked very much like my dad. Soon the grumbling started, and my face turned red as I tried to tighten the little screws into the trunk.

As much as I'd love for my children to have great fodder for personal essays when they're older, it would be nice for them to have a mom who isn't completely out of her mind the night we put up the Christmas tree. So I've tried to make things a little easier on all of us. Now, we buy the tree one day, put the lights on it another, and decorate it the day after that. On that day we have our party.

music to set the scene:

Cambridge Singers Christmas Album, by John Rutter and the Cambridge Singers
Sing We Christmas or *A Chanticleer Christmas,* by Chanticleer
When My Heart Finds Christmas, by Harry Connick Jr.

Our Tree Trimming Party is special. It's the first celebration we have for the Christmas season—before school parties, office parties, and Christmas concerts. With just the four of us, it's the perfect time to put the holiday in perspective and focus on what's most important before anyone from the outside can pull us from home.

Listening to carols is essential. We love anything Christmassy by Chanticleer, the choral group from San Francisco. We also love the Cambridge Singers, directed by John Rutter. After our dinner of Cranberry Glazed Ribs and Pear-y Cherry Crumble, and once the last ornament is placed, we turn off all the lights but those on the tree and start reading *A Christmas Carol*. We continue to read as much as we can each night so it's finished by Christmas Eve.

To kick off the holiday season with your own family—whether you celebrate Christmas, Chanukah, Kwanzaa, or any other holiday—decide what you wish your family to focus on for the upcoming weeks, whether it is giving, selflessness, family, or peace. As you eat dinner and decorate for the holidays, discuss what the holiday means to you, and encourage the children to do the same.

get creative:
Have children write about their favorite holiday traditions in their journals, or save what they write in a family album.

Cranberry Glazed Ribs

Pretty much any dish made with cranberries makes me happy. They are synonymous with the holidays and my childhood on the South Shore in Massachusetts. I couldn't think of a better way to eat them than blended into a sauce and simmered with a pot of short ribs. SERVES 8

1. Heat 1 tablespoon olive oil in a medium saucepan set over medium-low heat. Add onions and salt, and cook until tender, about 10 minutes. Stir in garlic, and cook 1 minute more. Add cranberries, brown sugar, vinegar, orange zest, and red pepper flakes. Cook until the cranberries pop and the sauce starts to thicken, about 10 minutes more.

2. Place the cranberry mixture in a blender while still warm. Cover the blender lid with a kitchen towel to manage splattering and protect your hands from the hot mixture. Blend until smooth.

3. Place remaining olive oil in a large skillet. Working in batches, brown the ribs on all sides. Transfer to the bottom of a slow cooker. Deglaze the skillet with a cup of water, and pour over the ribs. Cover with cranberry glaze. Cook on low for 8 hours. Serve with Light as Air Mashed Potatoes.

2 tablespoons olive oil

1 small yellow onion, finely chopped

1 teaspoon kosher salt

2 cloves garlic, chopped

2½ cups cranberries

¾ cup brown sugar

1 teaspoon balsamic vinegar

Zest of 1 orange

Pinch of red pepper flakes

2–3 pounds beef short ribs

Light as Air Mashed Potatoes

Everyone has their own favorite way to make mashed potatoes. Nearly every time I make them, I do something differently, whether it's adding a new ingredient—like cream cheese or caramelized onions—or trying a new technique.

Along the way, I have discovered that a food mill with a hand crank is the best tool for mashing potatoes. If you have one, you can skip the step of peeling the potatoes. Just leave the skins on, chop them, and add them to the pot. After the potatoes cook, add them to the food mill, and it will do the work of peeling and mashing for you. SERVES 8

7 medium Yukon Gold potatoes, peeled and cut into ½-inch slices

2 teaspoons kosher salt, plus more for seasoning

5 tablespoons butter, melted

¼–½ cup milk

Freshly ground black pepper

1. Place potatoes in a medium saucepan, and add enough water to cover them. Set over high heat, and bring to a boil. Add salt, and reduce heat to a bubbling simmer. Cook until potatoes are tender to the point of a knife. Drain potatoes.

2. Use a ricer, a food mill, or a potato masher (but not a blender or a food processor) to mash the potatoes. Stir in butter and a little bit of milk at a time, until the desired consistency is achieved. Season with salt and pepper to taste.

3. Transfer to the bowl of an electric mixer fitted with the whisk attachment, and whisk potatoes until light and fluffy.

Parker House Rolls

Parker House Rolls

There are at least a hundred versions of Parker House Rolls. This is mine. MAKES 3 DOZEN ROLLS

4 cups unbleached all-purpose flour

1 package (1 scant tablespoon) rapid yeast

3 tablespoons honey or brown rice syrup

1 teaspoon kosher salt

1½ cups warm milk (110°F)

4 tablespoons unsalted butter, melted, plus more for bowl

1 whole egg

3 egg yolks

1 stick (8 tablespoons) salted butter, melted

1. In the bowl of an electric mixer fitted with the dough hook, mix flour and yeast. Add honey, salt, milk, unsalted butter, egg, and egg yolks. Knead on low speed for 10 minutes, until the dough is smooth and elastic. The dough will be very sticky.

2. Turn dough out onto a well-floured board, and knead quickly a few times to pull into a soft, cohesive ball. Pour a little melted butter into the bottom of a large mixing bowl. Roll the dough around in the butter, and cover with plastic wrap. Let rise in a warm place until doubled in size, about 40 minutes. Punch down dough to redistribute bubbles. Let rest for 3 minutes.

3. Roll dough with a rolling pin on a well-floured board into an 18 x 24-inch rectangle. Use a pizza cutter or a sharp knife to cut the dough into 36 rectangles (6 rows of 6).

4. Dip the bottom half of a rectangle in the melted salted butter. Lay the buttered half down in the pan, and fold the other half up and over, so the unbuttered half faces up. Use your finger to press the top half into bottom half. Repeat with remaining pieces of dough, lining them up in rows, and slightly overlapping each row over the preceding one. Cover with a buttered piece of plastic wrap and let rise for 40 minutes, or until doubled in size.

5. Preheat oven to 350°F. Remove plastic and bake rolls for 12–18 minutes, or until golden brown. Brush tops of rolls with any remaining melted butter. Serve warm.

books to inspire:

A Christmas Carol, by Charles Dickens
The Gift of the Magi, by O. Henry
Elijah's Angel, by Michael J. Rosen

Pear-y Cherry Crumble

My favorite desserts in the world are fruit crumbles and crisps. This one uses pears, but they could easily be replaced with Granny Smith apples. SERVES 8

1. Preheat oven to 350°F. In a large bowl, combine pear chunks, cherries, sugar, and lemon juice. Place in a medium casserole dish.

2. In a separate large bowl, whisk all the topping ingredients except the butter. Add butter and use your fingers to break it up until mixture is well combined and clumps together. Form into a ball and crumble over the fruit.

3. Place the casserole dish on a cookie sheet to catch drips, and bake for 1 hour, or until pears are soft to the point of a knife and juices are bubbling.

For the filling:

8 ripe Bartlett pears, peeled and cut into 1½-inch chunks

1 cup dried tart cherries

½ cup sugar

2 tablespoons freshly squeezed lemon juice

For the topping:

1 cup unbleached all-purpose flour

½ cup almond flour, or ½ cup slivered almonds chopped up in a food processor

¼ cup brown sugar

¾ cup granulated sugar

½ teaspoon kosher salt

½ teaspoon ground cardamom

¼ teaspoon ground ginger

¼ teaspoon ground cloves

1½ sticks (12 tablespoons) cold unsalted butter, cut in pieces

index

about the author

Jaime Richardson grew up in a coastal town south of Boston, where she learned to value classical music, literature, long walks on beaches, and fried scallops. Her love of food photography began at Brigham Young University, where she earned a bachelor's degree in design and bought her first copy of *Martha Stewart Living* magazine.

When Jaime began her family, she became troubled by the amounts of artificial ingredients in the food readily available, and turned her attention to cooking and baking from scratch, learning the majority of her skills from cooking programs and food magazines. She rarely followed recipes exactly, and ended up creating many of her own original dishes. As a way to keep a record of the recipes she created, and as a place to share her musings on raising her children and share her love of all things sophisticated, she began her blog Sophistimom in July of 2008. Since that time, Sophistimom has earned awards from around the Web, including being named one of Babble.com's Top 100 Mommy Food Bloggers in 2010, 2011, and then again in 2012.

Sophistimom has earned the attention of The Pioneer Woman, where her food was featured on both ThePioneerWoman.com and TheTastyKitchen.com. She is featured in the book *Where Women Cook: Celebrate!: Extraordinary Women & Their Signature Recipes*. Her work has appeared on Gourmet Live, *Gourmet Magazine*'s daily blog; *Glamour Magazine*'s Health blog; and in *Dessert* magazine. Jaime was a food writer and photographer for Babble.com on their food blog, The Family Kitchen. Her recipes have appeared in *Martha Stewart's Everyday Food* magazine, as part of Newman's Own "Own It!" campaign. She is part of Martha's Circle, a small group of lifestyle bloggers, handpicked by the editors at Martha Stewart.

Jaime lives with her family near Salt Lake City, Utah.